MTEL
Early Childhood Practice Questions

MTEL Practice Tests & Review for the
Massachusetts Tests for Educator Licensure

Dear Future Exam Success Story:

First of all, **THANK YOU** for purchasing Mometrix study materials!

Second, congratulations! You are one of the few determined test-takers who are committed to doing whatever it takes to excel on your exam. **You have come to the right place.** We developed these practice tests with one goal in mind: to deliver you the best possible approximation of the questions you will see on test day.

Standardized testing is one of the biggest obstacles on your road to success, which only increases the importance of doing well in the high-pressure, high-stakes environment of test day. Your results on this test could have a significant impact on your future, and these practice tests will give you the repetitions you need to build your familiarity and confidence with the test content and format to help you achieve your full potential on test day.

Your success is our success

We would love to hear from you! If you would like to share the story of your exam success or if you have any questions or comments in regard to our products, please contact us at **800-673-8175** or **support@mometrix.com**.

Thanks again for your business and we wish you continued success!

Sincerely,
The Mometrix Test Preparation Team

TABLE OF CONTENTS

Practice Test #1

1. According to many experts, how much of a child's speech should his/her parents understand by the time the child is a given age?

    a. Parents should be able to understand half of their child's speech by the time s/he is 18 months.

    b. Parents should be able to understand half of their child's speech by the time s/he is 3 years old.

    c. Parents should be able to understand everything their child says by the time s/he is 2 years old.

    d. Parents should be able to understand nearly all a child's speech by the time s/he is 3 years old.

2. Which of the following typically develops in young children at the latest ages?

    a. Responding to stories by requesting frequent repetitions

    b. Responding to commands including two actions or stages

    c. Responding to simple "who"/"what"/"where" questions

    d. Responding to simple questions about stories they heard

3. Research has found that 75% of children can accurately articulate which of the following speech sounds at the youngest age?

    a. The initial "sh" sound in "shut"

    b. The initial "v" sound in "voices"

    c. The initial "r" sound in "radios"

    d. The initial "th" sound in "think"

4. Which Piagetian cognitive ability has the younger child not attained that the older child has?

    A younger child watches you pour juice from a short, wide container into a tall, thin container and concludes there is more juice in the taller container because s/he sees the juice rising up higher in the glass. An older child concludes there is the same amount of juice either way, pointing out, "This glass is taller than the other one, but it's also thinner. Besides, I just saw you pour it from that glass to this glass, so it's the same amount no matter what the glasses look like."

    a. Object permanence

    b. Volume conservation

    c. Formal operations

    d. Class inclusion

5. On their way to the "Correct" stage of spelling development, in which of the other four stages are children most likely to use invented spellings?

    a. Phonetic

    b. Transitional

    c. Semiphonetic

    d. Precommunicative

6. A young child, angry at one parent, momentarily wishes he would leave. Later, when that parent moves out as the couple separates, the child blames it on her earlier wish. Piaget called this:

    a. Animism
    b. Egocentrism
    c. Magical thinking
    d. Intuitive thinking

7. The older child pointed out having observed the juice being poured from one container to another. If you then poured it back into the first container and the child used the same logic to conclude it was still the same quantity, which ability defined by Piaget would this demonstrate?

    a. Object permanence
    b. Conservation of number
    c. Reversibility of operations
    d. Secondary circular reaction

8. Piaget's first stage of cognitive development involves:

    a. Operations with concrete things
    b. Sensory input and motor output
    c. Operations with abstract things
    d. Intuition and animism, not logic

9. Which process identified by Piaget allowed the older child to make his/her conclusion?

    a. Intuition
    b. Centration
    c. Classification
    d. Decentration

10. Of the following, which is most accurate about the timing of children's speech development?

    a. Children speaking fewer than 50 words by 18–24 months will always be needing therapy.
    b. Children speaking fewer than 50 words by 18–24 months may or may not need therapy.
    c. Children speaking fewer than 50 words by 18–24 months are normal, needing no therapy.
    d. Children speaking fewer than 50 words by 18–24 months in baby talk must have therapy.

11. Which behavior indicates a child has attained understanding of symbolic representation?

    a. Seeking unseen things
    b. Playing "make-believe"
    c. Enjoying "peek-a-boo"
    d. Addition using pennies

12. Through which process identified by Piaget did the younger child *most* make his/her conclusion?

    a. Intuition
    b. Operation
    c. Centration
    d. Decentration

13. At which ages do normally developing children typically recognize spoken words they hear that name familiar objects, questions, and requests?

    a. Around 4–6 months
    b. About 7–12 months
    c. Around 0–3 months
    d. From 12–24 months

14. Which substage of cognitive development defined by Piaget typically occurs latest?

    a. Coordination of Reactions
    b. Tertiary Circular Reactions
    c. Primary Circular Reactions
    d. Secondary Circular Reactions

15. When can normally developing children typically combine four or more words into sentences?

    a. Around 1–2 years old
    b. Around 2–3 years old
    c. Around 3–4 years old
    d. Around 4–5 years old

16. As young children develop speech, which of the following examples of normal phonological processes typically disappears at the latest age?

    a. Pronouncing "sleep" as "teep"
    b. Pronouncing "juice" as "goose"
    c. Pronouncing "thinks" as "tinks"
    d. Pronouncing "pig" as "pick"/"big"

17. Which of the following most represents expert guidelines for how much of a young child's speech should be comprehensible to strangers at different ages?

    a. Strangers generally can comprehend only about 10% of a child's speech at 1 year.
    b. Strangers generally find about 25% of a 2-year-old child's speech to be intelligible.
    c. Strangers can usually understand everything a child is saying by the age of 3 years.
    d. Strangers will likely not understand everything a child says until s/he is 4 years old.

18. In which of Piaget's stages of cognitive development is the older child?

    A younger child watches you pour juice from a short, wide container into a tall, thin container and concludes there is more juice in the taller container because s/he sees the juice rising up higher in the glass. An older child concludes there is the same amount of juice either way, pointing out, "This glass is taller than the other one, but it's also thinner. Besides, I just saw you pour it from that glass to this glass, so it's the same amount no matter what the glasses look like."

    a. Preoperational
    b. Concrete operations
    c. Sensorimotor
    d. Formal operations

19. In which of Piaget's stages of cognitive development is the younger child?

> A younger child watches you pour juice from a short, wide container into a tall, thin container and concludes there is more juice in the taller container because s/he sees the juice rising up higher in the glass. An older child concludes there is the same amount of juice either way, pointing out, "This glass is taller than the other one, but it's also thinner. Besides, I just saw you pour it from that glass to this glass, so it's the same amount no matter what the glasses look like."

    a. Sensorimotor
    b. Concrete operations
    c. Preoperational
    d. Formal operations

20. Which of the following is true of state legal regulation of medical care, policies and procedures in ECE settings?

    a. Being disease-free, passing TB tests, and accurate staff and child health records are omitted from state regulations.
    b. Staff's administering medication to children in ECE is not a part of state government childcare licensing regulations.
    c. When emergencies due to illness, injuries, and accidents arise, management by ECE staff is regulated by the states.
    d. Litigation is more likely for not reporting abuse/neglect than not making accident reports or following procedures.

21. Among four areas of medical care and treatment that are the focus of U.S. state government child care licensing regulations, which choice correctly reflects one area?

    a. State licensing regulations for ECE staff health requirements do not include testing.
    b. State licensing regulations prohibit ECE staff's administering medication to children.
    c. State licensing regulations dictate ECE staff's management of medical emergencies.
    d. State licensing regulations do not cover non-emergency treatments in ECE settings.

22. What statement is most accurate regarding how the ECE field addresses adult interactions?

    a. EC research includes extensive work on how adult collaboration influences children.
    b. EC educators need to use teamwork to foster safe, trustworthy climates for children.
    c. EC curriculum models and approaches do not address any interactions among adults.
    d. EC professional development and training often cover topics about adult interaction.

23. According to ECE experts, what is true about various teacher strategies to enhance communication between themselves and parents?

    a. Parents find it pretentious for teachers to attach business cards to letters they send.
    b. Parents feel pressured when teachers send them invitations to school Open Houses.
    c. Parents will expect communication more if the teacher publishes a class newsletter.
    d. Parents who get children's appreciation letters will not benefit, though children will.

24. Regarding interactions among adults in ECE settings, which of these is most appropriate?

    a. Sharing anecdotal observations of children within their program violates confidentiality.
    b. Problem-solving activity and dialogue help educators identify what and how to improve.
    c. Each teacher in an ECE program should be responsible for one classroom, and not share.
    d. ECE educators can share information, but they should not collaborate to plan instruction.

25. What statement is most correct about how research, theoretical literature, professional development do/do not address adult-adult interactions within ECE settings and/or how educators can do this?

    a. Research into ECE includes numerous studies of adult collaboration and how it influences children.

    b. The High/Scope curriculum model omits adult teamwork in planning lessons or sharing information.

    c. The Creative Curriculum does not address adult-adult interactions or sharing responsibilities in ECE.

    d. Sharing instructional goals and responsibilities as a team creates safe, trusting climates for children.

26. Which of the following is most accurate regarding educator interactions with other adults in ECE settings?

    a. Most ECE settings equally emphasize development of children's social skills and adult-adult relationships.

    b. Required staff meetings in ECE settings include ample concentration in nurturing adult-adult relationships.

    c. Adults interact equally in daily ECE classroom settings as during in-services and professional development.

    d. ECE professionals must make conscious efforts to communicate and collaborate with adults to meet goals.

27. If parents do not pick up children from an ECE center on time, what is true of the ECE center's legal responsibilities?

    a. ECE staff are more likely to incur legal liability keeping a child at the center.

    b. ECE staff are not likely to incur legal liability taking a child home with them.

    c. ECE staff must discuss reasons and solutions with chronically tardy parents.

    d. ECE staff should not tell the police if they must remove a child who was left.

28. Which of these is true about confidentiality of records in ECE settings?

    a. Records of children in special education are subject to FERPA, the IDEA, and state laws.

    b. Records of children in special education are subject to the IDEA, not FERPA or state law.

    c. Records of children are still subject to confidentiality laws if abuse/neglect is suspected.

    d. Records of children released by ECE employees reporting abuse or neglect incur liability.

29. Which of the following is correct regarding types of legal child custody?

    a. Physical custody confers more rights than legal custody.

    b. Legal custody confers more rights than physical custody.

    c. Physical and legal custody give different but equal rights.

    d. Legal custody entails immediate care but not long-term.

30. What best reflects things ECE center administrators can do if non-custodial/unauthorized adults come to pick up children?

    a. Inform the unauthorized adult of the center's policies and procedures regarding custody.

    b. They must not show the adult the custodial court order when informing them of policies.

    c. Notify the enrolling adult and write a report; meetings or other measures are unneeded.

    d. An administrator should call the police whether the unauthorized adult goes away or not.

31. Two preschoolers have been given equal amounts of milk. One child complains that the other has more than he does because the other child's milk is in a taller, thinner glass and looks like more to him. According to Piaget's theory of cognitive development, which adult response would be most effective?

    a. Make sure that both children have milk in identically sized and shaped glasses.
    b. Explain that the taller glass is also thinner, so both glasses hold equal amounts.
    c. Pour the milk from each glass into another to demonstrate the equal amounts.
    d. Pour the milk into measuring cups to show how many ounces each glass holds.

32. To apply Bandura's theory, educators must realize that he emphasized _____ as the most important influence on learning.

    a. Nuclear conflicts
    b. Erogenous zones
    c. Cognitive abilities
    d. Social interactions

33. Which of the following reflects the definition of content validity in a test?

    a. A test gets results similar to those of a similar, validated test.
    b. A test measures the complete domain it is meant to measure.
    c. A test gets results that accurately foretell behavior in real life.
    d. A test actually measures the construct it is meant to measure.

34. Which of these most accurately represents a characteristic of the Language Experience Approach (LEA) to literacy instruction?

    a. Children get to interact with published text in books.
    b. Children get to use their own experiences and words.
    c. Children get to write down the stories they compose.
    d. Children get to read text in books aloud to a teacher.

35. Jean Piaget, Erik Erikson, and John Dewey, among others, emphasized the philosophy of constructivism in their theories. Which of the following founders of ECE programs also did?

    a. Friedrich Froebel
    b. Each of these did.
    c. Maria Montessori
    d. David P. Weikart

36. Which of the following is correct regarding basal readers for teaching reading?

    a. Basal readers involve a top-down approach.
    b. Reading sub-skills are taught systematically.
    c. Sequencing of teaching sub-skills is flexible.
    d. These have become rare in the twenty-first century.

37. One ECE student's parents want to know if their child is gifted. Another student's parents want to know if their child has a developmental disability. A third student's parents want to know how well their child is mastering all areas of development. A fourth student's parents want to know if and how their child's mastery levels may have changed since last year. What kinds of tests should the educators give the children to answer these parents' questions?

a. Norm-referenced tests for the first and third child, criterion-referenced for the second and fourth

b. Norm-referenced tests for the first two children, and criterion-referenced tests for the other two

c. Criterion-referenced tests for the first two children, and norm-referenced tests for the other two

d. Criterion-referenced tests for the first and third child, norm-referenced for the second and fourth

38. In the Directed Reading Activity (DRA) approach to reading instruction using basal readers, the first of five steps is the teacher's preparing and motivating students to read, and introducing new concepts and vocabulary words. Which of the following shows the correct sequence of the other four steps?

a. Guided silent reading; comprehension discussion; reading aloud; workbook activities

b. Reading aloud; comprehension discussion; workbook activities; guided silent reading

c. Comprehension discussion; workbook activities; guided silent reading; reading aloud

d. Workbook activities; reading aloud; guided silent reading, comprehension discussion

39. Which of the following is NOT true about the whole language approach to literacy instruction?

a. The whole language approach is effective for children with language processing disorders.

b. The whole language approach is effective for supporting constructivist learning of literacy.

c. The whole language approach is effective for integrating literacy across content domains.

d. The whole language approach is effective for emphasizing cultural diversity in instruction.

40. Why are questionnaires and surveys appropriate to use as screening tools in ECE?

a. They require more training and are harder to administer but give more detail.

b. They give less detailed information but take less time than other instruments.

c. They cost more but are administered more easily than other assessment tools.

d. They cost less than other instruments but can only be used in certain settings.

41. Regarding basal reader texts, which of these is accurate?

a. They contain narrative, not exposition.

b. They contain exposition, not narrative.

c. They are organized thematically by unit.

d. They are not classified by reading level.

42. According to Carl Rogers, _____ lead(s) to _____, which in turn develops _____, which reflects the _____.

a. Conditions of worth; positive regard; positive self-regard; ideal self

b. Organismic valuing; conditions of worth; positive self-regard; real self

c. Organismic valuing; positive regard; positive self-regard; real self

d. Conditions of worth; conditional positive regard; positive self-regard; real self

43. When teaching young children, which of the following ideas most reflects Albert Bandura's Social Learning Theory?

    a. Children can only learn through social interaction with others.
    b. Children learn by doing and by observing and imitating others.
    c. Children must observe but need not remember to copy others.
    d. Children need no motive to observe, retain, and imitate others.

44. During Piaget's second stage of cognitive development, adults should realize that children's thinking is primarily:

    a. Logical
    b. Intuitive
    c. Sensory
    d. Motoric

45. In the Language Experience Approach (LEA) to beginning literacy, which of its four steps is performed by the children alone rather than by children and teacher together or by the teacher alone?

    a. The construction of sentences to form a story
    b. The choice of a topic to create a story about it
    c. The writing down of sentences making a story
    d. The final review of the complete story record

46. Which EC pioneer originated the concept of kindergarten?

    a. Maria Montessori
    b. Siegfried Engelmann
    c. Friedrich Froebel
    d. Lucy Sprague Mitchell

47. What statement is accurate about integrated ECE curricula using thematic units?

    a. Organizing by themes addresses groups rather than individual child differences.
    b. Organizing by themes affords many hands-on learning activities for preschoolers.
    c. Organizing by themes requires assessments other than portfolio or performance.
    d. Organizing by themes makes learning meaningful but excludes any benchmarks.

48. What is accurate regarding manipulative objects that can help young children learn math concepts?

    a. Teachers can find many math manipulatives for sale, and/or can make their own homemade ones.
    b. Teachers can only find helpful math manipulatives by buying those made by expert manufacturers.
    c. Teachers will save money and attain much greater learning benefits by hand-making manipulatives.
    d. Teachers should not waste money buying, or time making, these as children learn more from ideas.

49. Which of the following would be consistent with Maslow's theory?

a. Being loved is more important for children than safe homes are.
b. Self-esteem is less important than having ideal personal growth.
c. A sense of belonging to a family supersedes getting enough rest.
d. Children need to breathe clean air more than feel socially valued.

50. When comparing the Directed Reading Activity (DRA) approach and the Directed Reading-Thinking Activity (DR-TA) approach using basal readers for reading instruction, what accurately reflects one of the main differences between the two?

a. DR-TA includes more specific directions and materials; DRA has more flexibility.
b. DRA is better using only basal readers; DR-TA applies to other reading activities.
c. DR-TA questions require convergent thinking; DRA requires divergent thinking.
d. DRA does not pre-teach words or schedule specific skills teaching; DR-TA does.

51. Of the following, which ECE expert is/was *most* known for her agreement with Piaget's theory and beliefs about early childhood education, and especially that education's goal is children's moral and social as well as intellectual development?

a. Maria Montessori
b. Constance Kamii
c. Lucy S. Mitchell
d. Rhetta DeVries

52. Of the following, which is more typical of a screening instrument than an assessment instrument?

a. Interpreting scores by weighting various item values
b. Interpreting scores by reversing point values of items
c. Interpreting scores by comparisons to national norms
d. Interpreting scores by comparisons to a cut-off score

53. Which of these is true about the use of manipulatives for EC math learning?

a. Manipulatives are so effective for learning that some early math curricula require these.
b. Manipulatives help preschoolers with visual/haptic learning styles but not other children.
c. Manipulatives can help preschoolers learn concrete things rather than abstract concepts.
d. Manipulatives are fun, but preschoolers do not learn by seeing/touching/moving objects.

54. Which of the following reflects application of Freud's third stage of development to early childhood practices?

a. Not taking personally when a 4-year-old rejects the same-sex parent for the other-sex parent
b. Being careful during toilet-training of toddlers not to focus excessive attention on the process
c. Making sure that any objects that baby can reach and mouth are not dangerous or unsanitary
d. Not taking personally when 7-year-olds shift their attention from their parents to their friends

55. What is most accurate regarding formal and informal observations for the screening and assessment of EC populations?

a. Informal observations are less likely to need training for administration.
b. Formal observations are made of children's activities in natural settings.
c. Informal observations are conducted of children in structured activities.
d. Formal observations usually take less time than informal observations.

56. Erikson designated his stage of psychosocial development focused on the conflict of Initiative vs. Guilt as a period characterized by:

    a. Friends
    b. Hope
    c. Trust
    d. Play

57. Which of the following initiatives promoting early childhood education came first?

    a. Early Head Start
    b. Project Head Start
    c. Project Follow Through
    d. Elementary and Secondary Education Act

58. According to principles of behaviorism, which of the following is an example of negative reinforcement?

    a. Telling a child s/he can skip a chore s/he dislikes in return for going to bed on time
    b. Telling a child s/he must do a chore s/he dislikes in return for going to bed too late
    c. Telling a child s/he can do more of something s/he enjoys for going to bed on time
    d. Telling a child s/he can have less of something s/he enjoys for going to bed too late

59. Which kind of informal assessment can provide the most continuity in recording a pre-K child's progress in a given area or domain?

    a. Running records
    b. Anecdotal records
    c. Portfolio assessments
    d. Observational checklists

60. In Montessori schools, preschool-aged children engage in activities to learn about music, art, and science in which of the Montessori areas?

    a. Language
    b. The Sensorial area
    c. Practical Life area
    d. Cultural Subjects

61. An assessment instrument that gives the same score to two children with very different needs is most likely to lack which kind of reliability?

    a. Internal consistency reliability
    b. Parallel forms reliability
    c. Test-retest reliability
    d. Inter-rater reliability

62. What statement accurately reflects a principle of emergent literacy theory?

    a. Listening and reading develop before speaking and writing.
    b. Children reach certain ages when they are ready for reading.
    c. Literacy develops gradually over time with child development.
    d. Research finds that in EC literacy learning, function follows form.

63. Which of the following adult practices reflects an understanding of the Anal stage of Freud's theory of psychosexual development?

    a. Understanding babies need safe, sanitary things to put in their mouths
    b. Understanding the willfulness and stubbornness of behavior in toddlers
    c. Understanding preschoolers' focusing on one parent, then on the other
    d. Understanding why school children focus on friends more than parents

64. The youngest children in Piaget's stage of Concrete Operations are typically in:

    a. Toddlerhood
    b. Preschool
    c. Elementary school
    d. Middle school

65. Among the following, which statement applies most to applying assessment results in planning ECE instruction?

    a. Lesson plans should promote developmental guidelines rather than child interests.
    b. Tracking progress should be systematic, but need not follow developmental order.
    c. Organizing outlines of developmentally appropriate guidelines informs assessment.
    d. Added support should be enriched for children below class level, and 1:1 for above.

66. Of the following formal assessments, which is used primarily for planning instruction?

    a. The Brigance Diagnostic Inventory of Early Development
    b. The Infant-Toddler Developmental Assessment
    c. The Bayley Scale for Infant Development
    d. The Early Coping Inventory

67. When light passes between different transparent media, its speed is changed by the change in medium and it is refracted, as when a straw in a glass of water seems to break or bend at the waterline. The amount that a medium slows down the speed of light is the:

    a. Normal line
    b. Wavelength
    c. Index of refraction
    d. Angle of refraction

68. How are animals of the Mollusca phylum able to respire?

    a. Through gills
    b. Through a trachea
    c. Through lungs
    d. Through muscle contraction

69. Which states of matter are not fluids?

    a. Solids
    b. Plasma
    c. Liquids
    d. Gases

70. The following represents a simple food chain. What trophic level contains the greatest amount of energy?

$$tree \rightarrow caterpillar \rightarrow frog \rightarrow snake \rightarrow hawk \rightarrow worm$$

    a. Tree
    b. Caterpillar
    c. Hawk
    d. Worm

71. A pulley lifts a 10 kg object 10 m into the air in 5 minutes. Using this information, you can calculate:

    a. mechanical advantage
    b. efficiency
    c. energy conservation
    d. power

72. Which of the following represents a chemical change?

    a. Sublimation of water
    b. A spoiling apple
    c. Dissolution of salt in water
    d. Breaking a rock in half

73. Limestone is one example of which subtype of sedimentary rock?

    a. Clastic
    b. Organic
    c. Chemical
    d. Pegmatite

74. Two companion models, gradualism and punctuated equilibrium, dominate evolutionary theory. Which of the following statements is MOST consistent with the theory of punctuated equilibrium?

    a. Fossils show changes over large periods of time.
    b. Fossils showing intermediate characteristics may not necessarily be found.
    c. Speciation occurs gradually.
    d. Evolution is a slow, steady process.

75. Which of the following is true about how light is absorbed?

    a. The sky is blue because the atmosphere reflects only blue wavelengths.
    b. The sky is blue because the atmosphere absorbs only blue wavelengths.
    c. Glass is transparent to all of the frequencies of light within the spectrum.
    d. Wood, metal, and other opaque materials reflect all wavelengths of light.

76. Which of the following is true?

    a. Materials whose atoms have strongly bound electrons conduct.
    b. Materials whose atoms have loose electrons insulate electricity.
    c. Materials with free electrons block the conduction of electricity.
    d. Materials whose atoms feature tightly bound electrons insulate.

77. In the scientific process, which skill do children employ most when they see patterns and meaning in the results of experiments they make?
    a. Measurement
    b. Classification
    c. Inferences
    d. Prediction

78. Among these everyday activities of young children, which most helps them develop concepts of 1:1 correspondence?
    a. Seeing how many coins are in a piggy bank or children are in their group
    b. Distributing one item to each child in the group or fitting pegs into holes
    c. Dividing up objects into piles by their types or by having the same shape
    d. Transferring sand/rice/water among various container shapes and sizes

79. When young children build structures from blocks and then knock them down or take them apart, which of these science concepts are they learning?
    a. Concepts of shape
    b. Concepts of weight
    c. Part-whole relations
    d. Temporal sequences

80. Among the states of matter, water vapor is classified as:
    a. A gas.
    b. A solid.
    c. A liquid.
    d. A plasma.

81. How are igneous rocks formed?
    a. Years of sediment are laid down on top of each other and forced together
    b. Acid rain caused by pollution creates holes in metamorphic rocks
    c. Dust and pebbles are pressed together underground from Earth's heat and pressure
    d. Magma from a volcanic eruption cools and hardens

82. What happens to gas particles as temperature increases?
    a. The average kinetic energy decreases while the intermolecular forces increase.
    b. The average kinetic energy increases while the intermolecular forces decrease.
    c. Both the average kinetic energy and the intermolecular forces decrease.
    d. Both the average kinetic energy and the intermolecular forces increase.

83. In the scientific method, which of the following steps should come first?
    a. Formulating a hypothesis
    b. Asking a research question
    c. Conducting an experiment
    d. Reporting proof or disproof

84. In a popular set of six conflict-mediation/resolution steps for young children, the first step is to approach the conflict calmly, interrupting any hurtful behaviors; the second step is to acknowledge the children's feelings. Of the subsequent four steps, while comes first?

    a. Gather enough information about the conflict.
    b. Elicit potential solutions; help children pick one.
    c. Reiterate/state over again what the problem is.
    d. Provide the children with support as is needed.

85. According to family systems theory, which statement is accurate regarding family boundaries?

    a. Disengaged families have more restricted/closed boundaries.
    b. Enmeshed families place a greater value upon independence.
    c. Disengaged families are more open to considering new input.
    d. Enmeshed families have looser and more flexible boundaries.

86. Which of the following correctly shows the chronological progress in EC development of five levels of self-awareness?

    a. Identification, self-consciousness, differentiation, situation, permanence
    b. Situation, differentiation, self-consciousness, permanence, identification
    c. Self-consciousness, identification, differentiation, permanence, situation
    d. Differentiation, situation, identification, permanence, self-consciousness

87. Which of the following is/are accurate about individualistic vs. collectivist orientations of some world cultures?

    a. Latin American and African cultures are more often individualistic.
    b. Individualism is less common in Canadian and Australian cultures.
    c. Native American and Asian cultures are typically more collectivist.
    d. European and North American cultures tend to be more collectivist.

88. On a geographical map, which of the following requires using a ratio to interpret?

    a. The key or legend
    b. The compass rose
    c. The scale of miles
    d. The lines in a grid

89. According to psychologist Diana Baumrind, which of the parenting styles she identified is the ideal?

    a. Authoritarian
    b. Authoritative
    c. Uninvolved
    d. Permissive

90. Among the following, which is correct regarding some essential geography concepts?

    a. An example of absolute location is urban vs. rural land prices.
    b. Relative location equals the latitude and longitude of a place.
    c. Product and land prices are affected by geographical distance.
    d. Achievability relates to surface conditions and never changes.

91. What is accurate regarding popular conflict resolution approaches for young children?

    a. EC conflict mediation steps are similar to the steps of adult conflict mediation.
    b. Adults should listen to emotions children express but should not say anything.
    c. Adults should gather information about a conflict but not talk directly about it.
    d. Suggesting possible conflict solutions should be done by an adult, not children.

92. In developing self-awareness, which of these can infants take relatively the longest to achieve?

    a. Showing eye-hand coordination by systematically reaching for and touching things
    b. Telling apart video of themselves from video of others doing the exact same things
    c. Using their sitting, posture, and balance levels to regulate their reaching for things
    d. Telling videos of them apart from video of other babies dressed in the same things

93. Which of the following behaviors typically develops earliest in babies/toddlers/young children?

    a. Coordinating their peer-play behaviors
    b. Sharing toy/object activities with peers
    c. Prosocial, helping, and caring behaviors
    d. Creating "make-believe" play scenarios

94. What accurately reflects acculturation vs. assimilation?

    a. Ethnic groups' uniting to form a new culture is acculturation.
    b. A dominant culture's absorbing other cultures is assimilation.
    c. Assimilation is when cultures adopt traits from other cultures.
    d. When two or more cultures virtually fuse, this is assimilation.

95. Of the four parenting styles identified by psychologists, which one is found most likely to result in children who have problems with authority figures, poor school performance, and poor self-regulation?

    a. Authoritarian
    b. Permissive
    c. Authoritative
    d. Uninvolved

96. An adult places a sticker on a small child's face and then introduces a mirror. When the child sees the sticker in the mirror, s/he reaches toward her/his face to remove it rather than toward the mirror. Which level of self-awareness does this demonstrate?

    a. Permanence
    b. Differentiation
    c. Situation
    d. Identification

97. A typically developing child is shown a TV with live video of herself, and also shown adult researchers who are imitating the child's behaviors. The child can tell the difference between the video and the imitators. This child is most likely:

    a. A newborn
    b. Two years old
    c. Four to seven months
    d. Four to six months

98. Of the following, what is most accurate about how cultural expression influences human behavior?

    a. African-American culture has historically developed a strong oral tradition.
    b. Latin American culture has not influenced North American music or dance.
    c. Recent Asian immigrants immediately adopt American family organization.
    d. European-American policy has not affected Native American tribal culture.

99. The price of oil drops dramatically, saving soda pop manufacturers great amounts of money spent on making soda pop and delivering their product to market. Prices for soda pop, however, stay the same. This is an example of what?

    a. Sticky prices
    b. Sticky wages
    c. The multiplier effect
    d. Aggregate expenditure

100. What does the 10th Amendment establish?

    a. Any power not given to the federal government belongs to the states or the people
    b. The President is responsible for executing and enforcing laws created by Congress
    c. Congress has the authority to declare war
    d. The Supreme Court has the authority to interpret the Constitution

Answer Key and Explanations #1

1. D: Normally, parents should be able to understand about 25% of their 18-month-old child's speech, not 50% (A). By the time a child is 2 years old, parents should understand about 50%–75% of the child's speech, not all of it (C). By the time the child is 3 years old, parents should be able to understand 75%-100% of the child's speech (D), rather than only half of it (B).

2. D: Children typically want to hear the same story (or song, rhyme, game, etc.) repeated over and over many times (A) when they are between 1 and 2 years old. They usually can follow two-part directions (B), like "Take off your shirt and put it in the hamper," between 2 and 3 years of age. They typically can understand and respond to simple "who," "what," and "where" questions (C) when they are between 3 and 4 years old. Children can typically answer simple questions about stories they have heard (D) when they are between 4 and 5 years old.

3. A: According to some research studies, 75% of normally developing children could accurately pronounce the "sh" sound in "shut" by the age of 4 years. 75% of children could accurately pronounce the "v" in "voices" (B) by the age of 6 years. 75% of children could accurately pronounce the "r" in "radios" (C) by the age of 5 years. And 75% of children could accurately articulate the "th" in "think" (D) by the age of 8½ years.

4. B: The experiment described is like those Piaget conducted with children to prove his theory of cognitive development. Conservation is the realization that the amount of a substance (or the number of a collection of objects) remains constant despite differences in its appearance, like the volume of liquid regardless of the size and/or shape of the container holding it. Piaget found preoperational children, who cannot perform mental operations, do not understand this concept, while concrete operational children do. Object permanence (A) is the realization (usually by infants around 8–9 months old) that things still exist when out of their sight. Formal operations (C) involve the ability to perform mental operations with abstract concepts, unaided by having concrete objects to see and manipulate. Class inclusion (D) is the ability to categorize objects or concepts into groups based on common properties. Conservation and class inclusion both emerge during the stage of concrete operations.

5. A: The first stage of spelling development is precommunicative (D), when children may use alphabet letters but have no idea these represent speech sounds. In the second, semiphonetic (C) stage, children begin to understand the correspondences of letters to sounds and use basic logic, like spelling "you" as "U" or "why" as "Y." The third stage is the phonetic (A) stage, when children do not necessarily use conventional spelling, but represent every phoneme they hear in a word with a letter or letter group in a systematic and comprehensible way. This is when they are most likely to use invented or phonetic spellings. In the fourth, Transitional (B) stage, children begin to use visual instead of auditory spellings.

6. C: Piaget coined the term magical thinking to describe the illogical thought of young children when they believe their own internal thoughts or words cause external events to happen in the world. Animism (A) was what Piaget termed the belief of young children that inanimate objects have thoughts and feelings. Egocentrism (B) was what Piaget called the characteristic in young children of being unable to see things—literally and concretely, not just abstractly—from others' perspectives, and their belief that the world revolves around them. Intuitive thinking (D) is how Piaget generally described the thought of preoperational children who are not yet able to think using logic.

7. C: When children first begin to think logically, they can perform mental operations related to concrete objects. Another feature of this development is what Piaget called reversibility, i.e., the ability to reverse an operation. For example, if a child can perform addition by adding more pennies or beads to a group while counting each new larger quantity, the child can then reverse this operation to perform subtraction, removing objects from the group while counting each new smaller quantity. Object permanence (A) refers to the understanding children typically develop during the sensorimotor stage that things they have seen still exist even when they no longer see them. Conservation of number (B) is Piaget's term for conserving numerical quantity. For example, 12 pennies are still 12 whether spread far apart or clustered closely together. The scenario described involves conservation of liquid volume, not of number. Secondary circular reactions (D) comprise a substage of Piaget's sensorimotor stage when children repeat actions purposefully.

8. B: Piaget's first stage of cognitive development is called the sensorimotor stage. This is when infants respond to input they receive from the environment through their sensory organs by engaging in motor actions. When they realize how the environment then reacts to some of these actions, they respond again; this is called circular reactions. Operations with concrete things (A) occur during Piaget's third stage called concrete operations. Operations with abstract things (C) occur during Piaget's fourth and final stage called formal operations. Intuition and animism but not logic (D) occur during Piaget's second stage, which he called preoperational.

9. D: The younger child demonstrated centration (C) by focusing on only the greater height of the juice in the thinner container compared to its lower height in the wider one. The older child demonstrated the process of decentration, which emerges during the concrete operations stage, by being able to attend to both height and width at the same time. The older child did not arrive at his/her conclusion via intuition (A) but logic. Classification (C) is the ability to group items by similarity.

10. B: Children classified as "late talkers" by speech-language pathologists and other developmental specialists have expressive vocabularies (words they speak) of fewer than 50 words. However, this general rule does not mean they will always need therapy (A) to increase their vocabularies. Some children meeting this description will be diagnosed with clinically significant speech, language, and/or hearing problems; others will not. Some are simply "late bloomers" whose expressive vocabularies will catch up in time. Others, however, cannot be assumed to be normal and not needing therapy (C). Parents should thus consult a professional if a child speaks fewer than 50 words at around 18–24 months of age to determine whether a problem exists. However, speaking in "baby talk" at these ages *is* normal, so parents should not be concerned about imperfect pronunciation in a two-year-old (D).

11. B: When children engage in "pretend" or "make-believe" playing, as when they play "house" and pretend to be parents; pretend to be fantasy characters; or use toys to represent real persons, animals, machines, etc., they understand one thing can be used as a symbol to stand for something else, i.e., symbolic representation. When babies look for things they saw that were then hidden so they can no longer see them (A), they have attained object permanence. The emergence of this understanding that things out of sight still exist is also indicated by their enjoying playing "peek-a-boo" (C). (Infants without object permanence are truly surprised to see a hidden face reappear; those developing object permanence laugh with delight to see the face reappear; and those with fully developed object permanence may eventually lose interest in the game.) When children can add or subtract using pennies (D) or other concrete objects, this shows they have attained concrete operations, i.e., mental operations using concrete objects.

12. C: The younger child made his/her conclusion through the process of centration. Piaget coined this term to describe how preoperational children focus on only one property of an object at a time. In this case, the younger child observed only the height of juice in the taller, thinner container without noticing that it is narrower than the shorter, wider container. Similarly, preoperational children can see a cookie or an apple cut up into pieces and conclude the many pieces equal more than the single whole. Intuition (A) generally means knowing something without visible proof; Piaget called preoperational children's thinking intuitive, meaning not logical. However, his term centration more precisely defines the process of centrally focusing on only one of an object's properties. The process of an operation (B) is one Piaget found children cannot perform in the preoperational stage. Decentration (D) is the process children achieve when they no longer centrate on one property but can consider multiple aspects at once, in the stage of concrete operations.

13. B: Babies typically begin turning to look at parents upon hearing their voices between birth and 3 months of age (C), stop crying upon hearing familiar voices, and stop what they are doing to listen to an unfamiliar voice. At around 4–6 months (A) old, babies are typically responsive to the word "no" and to changes in parental tones of voice, as well as to nonvocal sounds. When they are about 7–12 months old, they recognize familiar spoken words for objects, people, questions, and requests (B). Children aged 12–24 months (D) can point to some body parts upon request and to pictures in a book upon hearing them named and can follow simple directions and understand simple questions.

14. B: From around 1–4 months of age, children engage in what Piaget called Primary Circular Reactions (C), wherein they may initially do something accidentally, and then repeat it later on purpose because they got pleasure from it before, like sucking their thumbs. From around 4–8 months old, children engage in Secondary Circular Reactions (D) by purposely repeating actions to interact with the environment, like picking up objects so they can mouth them. From around 8–12 months old, children are in the substage Piaget called Coordination of Reactions (A), when they perform actions with clear intention, like shaking a rattle to hear the sound. The latest substage, around 12–18 months old, is Tertiary Circular Reactions (B), when children experiment through trial and error to see what they accomplish, like which actions or sounds will best get parental attention. These are all Piaget's substages of his sensorimotor stage of cognitive development.

15. C: When children are around 1–2 years old (A), they typically can combine two words into questions and statements. When they are around 2–3 years old (B), they typically can make utterances combining up to three words. Around 3–4 years of age, they typically can combine four or more words. At around 4–5 years old (D), they typically can speak fluently and clearly in long, complex, compound, and complex-compound sentences.

16. C: Pronouncing "thinks" as "tinks" equals articulating a fricative as a stop. This normal phonological process typically disappears when children are about 5 years old. Pronouncing "sleep" as "teep" (A) equals the reduction of a consonant cluster to a single consonant; this typically disappears when children are around 4 years old. Pronouncing "juice" as "goose" (B) equals articulating an affricate (a combination of a stop like /d/ with a fricative like /ʒ/ to form /dʒ/, the "j" sound in "juice") as a stop—in this case, /g/. This normally disappears when a child is about 4½ years old. Pronouncing "pig" as "pick" equals devocalizing the final consonant, while pronouncing "pig" as "big" (D) equals pre-vocalic voicing, i.e., letting the voicing of the vowel sound transfer to a preceding unvoiced consonant like /p/, making it /b/. These normal phonological processes both typically disappear when children are about 3 years old.

17. D: Familiarity enables parents to understand their young children's speech better when the children are younger than when strangers can understand the same proportions of their speech.

According to a number of experts, strangers can usually understand about 25% of a 1-year-old's speech, not 10% (A). Of 2-year-old children's speech, about 50% is typically intelligible to strangers, not 25% (B). Whereas parents may understand all or most of what their 3-year-olds say, strangers usually understand only about 75% of it, not everything (C). Strangers will not understand everything uttered by young children until they are around 4 years old (D).

18. B: The older child has reached the stage of concrete operations because s/he can understand by observing the juice being poured from one glass to another that the amount of juice has not changed even though the shapes of the containers differ. Children in this stage of cognitive development can think logically, as long as they can also perform the operation concretely using real objects, and can see real, concrete proof of that logic. Children in the preoperational (A) stage cannot yet perform mental operations, even when they have concrete objects to see and manipulate. Children in the sensorimotor (C) stage develop mentally through physical means, i.e., receiving sensory input and responding to it by creating motor output. Children in the stage of formal operations (D) can perform mental operations with abstract concepts, without needing any concrete objects to look at or to manipulate.

19. C: The younger child cannot yet perform concrete operations like conservation of liquid volume, so this child is still in Piaget's preoperational stage. Children in this stage think intuitively rather than logically. The sensorimotor (A) stage is when babies typically learn about the world by receiving sensory information from their environments, respond through motor activities, and learn more by discovering not only what their bodies can do, but also how the environment reacts to their actions. The stage of concrete operations (B) typically emerges in middle childhood, enabling children to perform logical mental operations like adding, subtracting, etc., by manipulating concrete objects. The stage of formal operations (D) typically emerges before or during adolescence, enabling children to understand and manipulate abstract ideas without the accompaniment of concrete objects.

20. C: One area that state government childcare licensing regulations address is how ECE staff manage emergencies caused by illness, injuries, and accidents. Another area they cover is employee health requirements including being disease-free, passing TB tests, and keeping accurate record of both staff and child health (A). A third area covered by these regulations is the administration of medications by staff to children in ECE settings (B). ECE settings must keep written policies and procedures for emergency and non-emergency care to protect children's health and safety; and to avoid litigation, their staff must scrupulously follow these. Lawsuits are equally likely for not reporting suspected or observed child abuse or neglect as for not completing accident reports or not following the written policies and procedures (D).

21. C: U.S. state licensing regulations for ECE settings focus on four areas. One is health requirements for all ECE staff, which includes not having communicable diseases or health conditions that would interfere with active child care; keeping accurate health records on both employees and children; and passing a TB test (A). The second area covers ECE staff's administration of medication to the children (B) they serve. The third area is management of medical emergencies (C) from illness, injury, and accident. The fourth area does cover ECE staff's non-emergency treatment (D) of minor illnesses, injuries, and accidents.

22. B: Very little research in the ECE field addresses how collaboration among adults influences the children they teach (A). However, there are some ECE curriculum models and approaches that do address interactions among adults (C); e.g., the High Scope curriculum, the Creative Curriculum, etc., primarily by pointing out that planning instruction and sharing responsibilities and information rely on teamwork among educators. Unlike ECE curriculum models but like ECE research literature, professional development and training programs in the field rarely cover or teach adult conflict resolution, how to work collaboratively, or adult learning principles (D). Thus, EC educators must themselves consciously apply teamwork, collaborative planning, and sharing of instructional goals and information toward supporting children's positive development.

23. C: ECE experts recommend various strategies for teachers to enhance their communication with parents. They find that when teachers attach their business cards to their first parent letters at the beginning of the school year, parents see the teachers as more professional, not pretentious (A). They find parents will be more likely to attend school Open Houses, feel more comfortable in classrooms, and see teachers as more approachable when teachers send them invitations, which parents do not tend to perceive as pressure (B). When teachers publish class newsletters weekly or monthly via internet sites, e-mails, or print to give parents informal updates on children's instruction and learning, parents learn to expect communication from teachers more (C). When teachers have children write their parents letters of appreciation for school Open Houses, the children are encouraged to invite their parents; plus, the parents also appreciate the teachers (D) by association with the children's appreciation.

24. B: When EC educators engage together in problem-solving activities and dialogues, this helps them identify what learning goals and experiences they can improve and how to do this to the children's benefit. It does not violate confidentiality to share anecdotal observations of children with other teachers within the same ECE program (A); this can better inform all teachers' instructional planning when each teacher bases plans on collective contributions instead of only on individual experiences. This also promotes positive interactions among the teachers. ECE professionals should also support each other by discussing and deciding together how to share their responsibilities (C) for teaching, arranging class projects, rearranging classrooms when needed, caring for class pets and plants, etc. ECE educators can not only share information and exchange ideas about children, their families, and instructional methods, but they can and should also collaborate in their instructional planning (D). This enhances both the interactions among educators and the effectiveness of their instruction.

25. D: ECE professionals must consider how their adult-adult interactions can support children in developing competence, capability, and confidence. When they share their instructional goals, plan learning experiences to support those goals, and share responsibilities as a team in implementing projects, they establish climates of safety and trust for children. Their responsibility to do these things is even more important, because research into ECE includes very little about adult collaboration and its influence on children (A). However, the High/Scope curriculum model does stress the importance of teamwork for planning lessons and sharing information (B) and responsibilities. The Creative Curriculum and similar models also address adult-adult interactions (C) in this way.

26. D: ECE experts find that teachers must work consciously to communicate and collaborate with other adults in their planning and daily classroom activity in order to meet their educational goals. This is because most ECE settings emphasize developing children's social skills with peers, but usually do not give equal emphasis to developing adult-adult relationships (A). Mandatory staff meetings in ECE settings are commonly preoccupied with curriculum and administration rather than with nurturing adult-adult relationships (B). While adults interact with each other during in-service trainings and professional development courses, they do not interact as much in daily ECE classrooms (C).

27. C: Legally, ECE centers are responsible for the welfare of children on their premises. If parents do not pick up their child and much time has elapsed, ECE staff are *less* likely to incur legal liability if they keep the child at the center (A) and *more* likely to incur legal liability if they take the child home with them (B). If it is impossible for staff and child to stay at the center and staff must remove a child who was left, the staff *should* inform the police (D) they are doing so and where they are taking the child to protect themselves from potential liability. If parents exhibit a chronic pattern of being tardy picking up their children, ECE staff must talk with them about why and what solutions are possible (C) because ECE employees are legally responsible to report it if they suspect child neglect.

28. A: The Family Educational Rights and Privacy Act (FERPA) governs the confidentiality of records on children in ECE settings. However, the records of children with disabilities who receive special education services in ECE settings—as such mainstreaming is increasingly common—are subject to the regulations of not only the FERPA, but also of the Individuals with Disabilities Education Act (IDEA) and the special education laws of the state where they are located rather than only the IDEA's regulations (B). One exception to the laws governing the confidentiality of student records is when abuse or neglect of a child is suspected; in this case, child abuse and neglect laws supersede FERPA and other confidentiality regulations (C). ECE employees are legally required to report suspected abuse and neglect, and they are also legally immune from liability (D) for doing so.

29. B: The law defines physical custody as the right and responsibility of an individual or agency to provide immediate care and housing in the present and immediate future, and legal custody as the right of an individual or agency to make decisions for a child about residence, medical treatment, and education. Physical custody does not confer as many rights as full legal custody (A), which affords the adult more rights (B). Thus, the rights of physical and legal custody are different but not equal (C). Physical custody, not legal custody, is more concerned with immediate care (D).

30. A: Current documentation of a child's custody arrangements should always be on file with dated signatures of the enrolling adult(s) at ECE centers. If a non-custodial/unauthorized adult comes to pick up a child, an ECE administrator should inform him/her of the center's policies and procedures regarding custody. The administrator may show this adult the copy of the custodial court order (B) if needed to convince the adult to desist. Administrators must notify the enrolling adult of any such incident; write a report; meet with the custodial adult(s) to review/update/clarify the child's current custody arrangements; document the meeting with signatures and date; and file this documentation in the child's record (C). These are all advisable if the unauthorized adult goes away; but if s/he refuses to go away, makes a scene, or threatens or shows violence, the ECE administrator can also call the police. Calling the police is not necessary if the adult goes away (D).

31. A: According to Piaget's theory, preschoolers are in his Preoperational stage of cognitive development when they cannot yet think logically. Piaget found Preoperational children "centrate" on only one property at a time, e.g., the height of liquid in a glass but not its width. Therefore it will do no good to explain to the child that the thinner width of one glass makes up for its greater height (B), as he will not understand this. Piaget and others after him have found that even demonstrating by pouring the milk into a differently sized and/or shaped container (C), though this seems visually obvious to adults and older children, does not prove anything to Preoperational children as they focus only on what they see, and on only one aspect of it. Likewise, showing them numerical measurements of ounces (D) is something they cannot yet understand. The most effective solution for children this age is simply to ensure both children have identically sized and shaped glasses.

32. D: Bandura's Social Learning Theory places emphasis on social interactions as the most important context of, and influence on, learning. Bandura says children learn by observing and then imitating others' behaviors. Nuclear conflicts (A) were Erikson's term for the central crisis to be resolved in each of his psychosocial stages of development. Erogenous zones (B) were Freud's term for areas of the body where children's attention focused in each of his psychosexual stages of development. Cognitive abilities (C) were the focus of each of Piaget's stages of cognitive development.

33. B: Content validity in a test instrument means that the test measures the full range of the domain or construct that it is intended to measure, rather than only part(s) of it. Choice (A) reflects the definition of concurrent validity in a test. Choice (C) reflects the definition of predictive validity in a test. Choice (D) reflects the definition of construct validity in a test.

34. B: The LEA lets children use their own life experiences in constructing stories, and enables them to use their own words in composing these. In this method, children are not interacting with published text in books (A) but creating their own. The LEA teaches beginning reading. When it is applied with young children, they are not writing down the stories they compose (C), the teacher is. They are not reading books aloud to the teacher (D); rather, they are dictating to a teacher, who transcribes what they say. Teachers and children then review the story they have created, and the teacher has recorded, together.

35. B: Froebel (A), Montessori (C), and Weikart (D) all embraced the philosophy of constructivism in the ECE programs they founded, as well as Mitchell in her Bank Street Curriculum and many others. Constructivism is the belief that we construct our own realities, and that by extension, in their education children also construct their own learning experiences. This philosophy influences the types of teaching approaches and methods used in ECE by providing children with opportunities for direct, hands-on, experiential learning through exploration, inquiry, discovery, the scientific method, practical applications of learning in real life, and lifelong learning.

36. B: The basal reader approach is bottom-up in nature, not top-down (A); i.e., sub-skills for reading are taught from smaller to larger parts and parts to whole. Students are aided in transitions from the part to the whole through instruction in a systematic (B) sequence that is followed rigidly, and is not flexible (C). While fewer publishers have issued basal reading series in the twenty-first century than in the twentieth, the basal reader approach to teaching reading is still the most common one in America: approximately 75% to 85% of classrooms in grades K–8 still use basal readers, so they are not at all rare (D). Other than the number of publishers offering them, the main difference is that previous basal reading series before/during the twentieth century emphasized vocabulary control and skill acquisition at the expense of comprehension and pleasure; whereas twenty-first-century basal readers enhance student motivation to read more with multiple versions of stories, book excerpts enabling selection sharing, and other sources of greater variety.

37. B: Norm-referenced tests compare a student's scores to the scores of a sample of students that are representative of the population for the same age, developmental level, or grade. They show how a student's performance compares to the average and whether that student is achieving significantly above or below the norm. Therefore, to tell parents if their children perform above average and may be gifted or below average and may have developmental disabilities, educators would administer norm-referenced tests. Criterion-referenced tests compare a student's scores to a performance standard for the student's age, developmental level, or grade, which has been pre-determined by educational experts. They show how a student's performance compares to established standards. To tell parents if their children have mastered all areas of development or whether and how children's mastery levels have changed over time, educators would administer criterion-referenced tests.

38. A: In the DRA approach, after teacher preparation and motivation of students and introduction of new concepts and vocabulary words, in the second step, students read silently with questions and statements from the teacher guiding their reading. In the third step, teacher and students discuss what they have read to develop student reading comprehension. In the fourth step, students read aloud. They also read answers aloud to questions the teacher has asked; this is called "purposeful rereading." The fifth step involves follow-up activities and practicing that students do using the companion workbooks to the basal readers. In some cases, there may also be enrichment activities that relate the reading to writing, art, drama, or music experiences.

39. A: The whole language approach, as its name implies, is holistic in nature and founded on constructivist principles; it supports children in constructing their own knowledge and meaning through interacting with their environments (B). This approach does emphasize the integration of literacy instruction across the various subject content domains (C). It also emphasizes cultural diversity in learners, instruction, and learning (D). However, because it is holistic rather than analytical like phonics, the whole language approach is NOT as effective for children who have language processing disorders and/or reading disorders because they require explicit instruction to learn the decoding skills and strategies that other children learn incidentally as they learn to read and write.

40. B: Questionnaires and surveys, which parents and other adults can complete with pencil and paper, are appropriate as screening tools in ECE because they require little training to administer (A). Though they yield less detailed information than other assessment instruments, they also take less time to complete (B). They often cost less than other assessment instruments as well as being easier to administer and complete (C), and they can be used in many different settings (D) like waiting rooms at pediatricians' offices, at home, in preschools, etc. Screening instruments need not provide the most comprehensive or detailed information. Other instruments that do are used for diagnosing and for developing individual plans of child care and instruction.

41. C: Basal reader texts are organized according to unifying themes for each unit. Basal readers include both narrative (A) AND exposition (B), as well as many different genres including children's literature. In addition, the texts supplied in basal reader series are all graded according to each reading level (D). This enables teachers to instruct students in reading by following the exact, systematic sequences prescribed, both for teaching reading sub-skills from bottom to top/smaller to larger, and for teaching students according to their current levels of reading.

42. C: Rogers said organismic valuing—i.e. valuing what is healthful—leads to positive regard—i.e. esteem for another; which in turn develops positive self-regard in the other person; which reflects the real self—i.e. the person one becomes under optimal conditions. Conditions of worth {(A), (B), and (D)} are what Rogers called externally imposed conditions society requires people to meet in order to value them. Rogers said these conditions of worth lead to conditional positive regard (D), i.e. only valuing individuals if they meet those conditions. He believed conditional positive regard develops conditional positive self-regard in individuals, which reflects the ideal self (A)—i.e. an unattainable self, based on others' standards—instead of the real self.

43. B: In developing his Social Learning Theory, Bandura found that children not only learn by doing, but also by observing others and imitating what they do. While Bandura emphasized the importance of the role of social interaction in learning, he never claimed children learn only through social interaction (A). Rather, he greatly extended what we know about children's learning potential by showing they can learn vicariously, through observation of others being rewarded for certain behaviors and imitating those behaviors to obtain similar rewards, as well as through direct experiences of receiving reinforcements for behaviors. Bandura defined four necessary conditions for social learning: they must attend to another's behavior; they must retain or remember what they observe (C); they must be able to reproduce or copy the behavior; and they must be motivated (D) to do the other three.

44. B: During Piaget's second, Preoperational stage, toddlers and preschoolers' thinking is primarily intuitive, as opposed to being logical (A); logic does not develop until later. Primarily sensory (C) and motoric (D) bases of thought are more closely associated with Piaget's first, Sensorimotor stage of cognitive development during infancy.

45. A: In the LEA's first step, the children and teacher collaborate to choose a topic of interest about which to compose a story (B). In the second step, the children alone take turns, each contributing one sentence at a time in their own words to advance the story's progress (A). The teacher alone transcribes in writing everything the children dictate during this step (C). During the children's oral composition and the teacher's written recording, the teacher stops after every several words or every few sentences and reads the record aloud for the children to confirm its accuracy in the third step. In the fourth step, when the story is completed, the teacher and children perform a record review together (D), with the teacher pointing to each word. Either the teacher and children read aloud together, or the teacher reads each word aloud and the children repeat, depending on the children's ability.

46. C: Friedrich Froebel (1782–1852) originated the concept of kindergarten ("children's garden" in German). Play-based instruction and the role of schools in social skills development were among the many influences of his educational theory. Maria Montessori (A) developed the Montessori Method of instruction; Montessori schools following her principles of hands-on, experiential learning operate today in multiple countries. Siegfried Engelmann (B) founded an important preschool program together with Carl Bereiter; revisited part of Piaget's theory and experiments with different results; developed the Direct Instruction philosophy and methods; collaborated with the Head Start and Follow Through Projects; and, with Wesley Becker, conducted the largest controlled study comparing ECE models. Lucy Sprague Mitchell (D) founded the Bank Street Curriculum and its Developmental Interaction Approach to ECE, emphasizing the direct, constructivist, and multifaceted nature of learning.

47. B: When teachers design integrated ECE curricula organized around themes, they can not only use themes that appeal to young children, they can also address individual differences among children (A), including individual strengths in various learning modalities. Approaching unit planning thematically offers many natural opportunities to offer hands-on learning activities for young children (B). A thematic approach to the integrated curriculum is also readily adaptable to being evaluated through portfolio assessments and performance-based assessments (C). Thematic organization of curriculum units make learning more meaningful to young children, while still allowing teachers to couch specific benchmarks for learning concepts and skills by age and/or developmental level within themes of interest to children (D).

48. A: It is possible for teachers to use effective manipulative objects to instruct young children in early math concepts by purchasing, constructing, and finding them. Geometric shapes, linking cubes, magnetized numbers and boards; weights and scales; math games and blocks; tangrams; color tiles; flash cards; play money and working toy cash registers, etc., can be bought from stores, catalogs, and online. Teachers can also construct useful math manipulatives from everyday materials, and they can use found objects without further assembly, like pebbles, seashells, buttons, bottle caps, keys, cardboard tubes, coffee stirrers, etc. It is not true that either buying (B) or making (C) manipulatives is superior; teachers can do one, the other, or both depending on budgets, time, availability, and preference. Young children learn best when ideas are embodied in concrete physical objects they can look at, touch, and handle, rather than when ideas are presented to them abstractly (D).

49. D: Maslow's humanistic theory centered on his Hierarchy of Needs, presented visually as a pyramid. The most fundamental needs are at the base of the pyramid, progressing to the highest needs at the tip. Maslow posited that the most basic needs must always be met before any higher level(s) of needs could be met. Physiological needs are at the bottom of the pyramid and must be met first; security needs are second; social needs third, esteem needs fourth, and self-actualizing needs fifth, at the top. Therefore, safe homes [security] come before being loved [social needs] (A). Self-esteem [esteem needs] comes before ideal personal growth [self-actualizing needs] (B). Getting enough rest [physiological needs] precedes belonging to a family [social needs] (C). Breathing clean air [physiological needs] precedes feeling socially valued [esteem needs] (D).

50. B: The DRA approach is meant to be used with basal readers and includes more specific guidelines, materials, questions, and directions; the DR-TA approach has fewer directions, gives teachers more responsibility and flexibility (A) in lesson planning, and thus can be used both with basal readers and also for lesson plans in other curriculum areas that include reading. The questions in DRA manuals are literal and factual, requiring convergent thinking; DR-TA questions require divergent, creative thinking as well (C). DRA does pre-teach vocabulary words before reading, and does indicate when to teach which reading comprehension skills. DR-TA does not pre-teach vocabulary, requiring more student decoding, and does not tell teachers when different comprehension skills should be taught, requiring teachers to be better at questioning and accepting alternative student responses (D).

51. B: Constance Kamii studied extensively with Jean Piaget and has attributed all explanations for child development to the cognitive-developmental theory of Piaget. She has done much work on applying Piaget's theory in EC settings. Maria Montessori (A) agreed with Piaget, and also with John Dewey and others; she formed her own ECE method and schools. Lucy S. Mitchell (C), who founded the Bank Street Curriculum and its Developmental Interaction Approach, based her methods on the theories of Piaget, Erikson, Dewey, and others. Rhetta DeVries (D) collaborated with Constance Kamii in forming the Kamii-DeVries Constructivist Perspective preschool educational model. DeVries thus also agreed with Piaget's theory; but Kamii is *most* known for exclusively applying Piaget's theory in a model for ECE.

52. D: Screening instruments are typically more likely to be simpler to score and interpret, often being possible to complete right after administration for sharing with stakeholders. Screening instruments are often used to indicate whether further assessment is needed. Assessment instruments are typically more thorough and involve more complicated scoring and interpretation that take longer. Results and interpretations can be shared with stakeholders later in scheduled meetings. Some techniques common in standardized assessment instruments include interpreting scores by reversing the point values of some items (B); by comparing a student's scores to tables showing the national norms (C) for students of the same age or grade level; and/or converting raw scores (the actual numbers the administrator gave to student responses) to standardized scores or percentages. In contrast, interpreting scores on screening instruments can be as simple as comparing them to a designated cut-off score (D) for further assessment.

53. A: It is true that manipulative objects have been found so effective for young children's learning that Horizons and other early math curricula actually require their use. Manipulatives that children can see, feel, and work with not only help young children who learn best through visual, tactile, and kinesthetic modalities, but they also help other young children (B) because young children's learning is mainly via looking at, touching, holding, arranging, and moving concrete things as well as being fun (D). Young children mostly do not understand abstract concepts yet, and are even less likely to understand them when presented in abstract form, but they are more able to access some abstract ideas that are presented in concrete forms (C).

54. A: Children of preschool ages are in Freud's third, Phallic stage of psychosexual development. Freud theorized in this stage, boys undergo the Oedipal conflict; neo-Freudians theorized girls undergo the Electra conflict. In each, children subconsciously fear retaliation from same-sex parents against the child's unconscious desire for opposite-sex parents. Little boys prefer Mommy, little girls Daddy. (In what he termed "identification with the aggressor," Freud/neo-Freudians said children resolve these conflicts by preferring and imitating same-sex parents.) (B) applies Freud's second, Anal stage of development. Making too much of the toilet-training process can result in the child's fixation in this stage. The results are either "anal-retentive" preoccupation with cleanliness, order, and detail; or conversely, "anal-expulsive" rebellion against authority, and/or messy behaviors. (C) applies Freud's first, Oral stage, when nursing babies learn about the world through their mouths. (D) applies Freud's fourth, Latency stage, when children's relationship focus shifts from parents to friends/classmates.

55. A: ECE personnel may use formal and/or informal observations to screen and assess children in their populations. Formal observation instruments more often require staff training to administer them than informal observations do (A). Formal observations involve observing children participating in activities that were structured for a particular instrument (B), whereas informal observations involve observing children's activities in natural settings (C) like the home or the preschool during playtime. Formal observational instruments often take more time than informal observations (D), averaging more than 20 minutes to administer. Informal observation can take shorter or longer times depending on the observer, child, and activity, but formal observation instruments rarely take less than 20 minutes.

56. D: Erikson's nuclear conflict and stage he termed Initiative vs. Guilt is associated with preschool ages (i.e. around ages 3-5 years old). Erikson called this stage the "play age," because children these ages have developed the ability to use symbols; e.g. using toys/objects to represent other objects, and people (like children) to represent other people (like adults); and engage in "make-believe"/pretend play (a development also noted by Piaget in his theory). Children take Initiative to plan and enact pretend roles and scenarios. Erikson's stage of Industry vs. Inferiority, coinciding with elementary school ages, focuses on friends (A) and school. Erikson identified hope (B) as a positive outcome of resolving the conflict of Basic Trust (C) vs. Mistrust in his first stage during infancy.

57. B: Project Head Start was launched in 1965 as part of President Lyndon B. Johnson's War on Poverty initiative. It has been repeatedly expanded and reauthorized in subsequent years. Project Follow Through (C) was begun in 1967, also as part of the War on Poverty, after it was discovered that the gains experienced by children in Head Start programs often did not last. Project Follow Through undertook a massive examination of instructional methods to discover how to extend Head Start programs' benefits to disadvantaged children for longer times, and ultimately to improve education. A reauthorization in 1994 of the original Head Start enabled the establishment of Early Head Start (A) to help children prenatally by serving pregnant women, and to serve infants and toddlers younger than 3 years. President William B. Clinton authorized grants for Early Head Start in 1995. The Elementary and Secondary Education Act was also begun in 1965 by Johnson, but did not directly focus on early childhood issues (D).

58. A: In behavioral terms, the word "negative" does not mean bad, but rather the subtraction of something as it does in mathematics. "Positive" does not mean good in behaviorism, but rather the introduction of something. Reinforcement is strengthening the probability of repeating a behavior when the event immediately following the behavior, or consequence, is something the individual emitting the behavior desires. Punishment is weakening the probability of repetition of a behavior when its consequence is undesirable. Hence, removing something a child dislikes to reward desired behavior constitutes negative reinforcement. Assigning a disliked chore for not going to bed on time (B) constitutes positive punishment, i.e., introducing an undesirable consequence for undesired behavior. Bestowing a privilege/reward for following rules (C) constitutes positive reinforcement, i.e., introducing a desirable consequence for desired behavior. Withholding a privilege for not following rules (D) constitutes negative punishment, i.e., removing a desirable consequence for undesired behavior.

59. A: Anecdotal records (B) provide valuable information that may not be captured in forms that teachers fill out for other informal assessments, but they are most often reports of occasional events or observations. Portfolio assessments (C) compile children's work products over periods of time, offering first-hand records of progress and cumulative assessments, but still limit evaluation of progress to separate examples created at separate points in time. Observational checklists (D) completed at regular intervals also show progress and/or change over time, but again only as snapshots of particular moments. Running records (A), however, are the most continuous of the informal assessments named.

60. D: Montessori schools are divided into five areas: Practical Life, Sensorial, Language Arts, Mathematics and Geometry, and Cultural Subjects. In the Language (A) area, children learn beginning literacy, including phonics and stories. In the Sensorial area (B), young children experience learning through the modalities of vision, hearing, touch, smell, and taste. In the Practical Life area (C), children learn skills for daily living activities like buttoning, zipping, meal preparation, cleaning up, etc. In the Cultural Subjects (D) area, young children learn early concepts and information about music, art, science, time, movement, geography, history, and zoology.

61. A: Internal consistency reliability means that a test's items correlate with one another and with the test's overall score, so they all measure the intended construct or area accurately. If two children with very differing needs score the same on the same test, their scores may come from different individual items on the test that do not correlate well with other items or the test overall. Parallel forms reliability (B) means that two different forms or versions of the same test yield the same scores when each is given to the same students. Test-retest reliability (C) means that a test will yield similar scores when given to a student and then re-administered to the same student a short time later. Inter-rater reliability (D) means that a test gives the same student similar scores when given at the same time and in the same setting but by different administrators.

62. C: Emergent literacy theory reflects research findings that as children grow and develop, their literacy gradually develops commensurately. This theory replaces the historically earlier idea of reading readiness, which assumed that children's development included a time period when they were ready for reading (B). Research supporting emergent literacy theory has found that although reception precedes expression with spoken language—i.e., listening comprehension develops ahead of speech production—this is not true with written/printed language: preschoolers find early writing activities easier than early reading activities. Hence (A) is incorrect. Research underlying emergent literacy theory has also found that function does NOT follow form (D). Form follows function: rather than learning literacy skills abstractly and in isolation and later applying them in life, young children primarily learn literacy through real-life activities that are functional, goal-directed, and meaningful so the application requires the learning rather than vice versa.

63. B: Understanding babies need to mouth things to learn about the world orally (A) reflects Freud's Oral stage of development. In this stage, Freud said learning is influenced by the oral focus of early nursing activity. Understanding willful and stubborn behavior in toddlers (B) reflects Freud's Anal stage, when they are becoming toilet-trained, learning to control their bodies, and to assert individual will. Understanding why preschoolers first focus on the opposite-sex parent, and later on the same-sex parent (C) reflects Freud's Genital stage. At this time, Freud said about boys, and neo-Freudians added about girls, that they undergo Oedipal and Electra conflicts of unconscious impulses of desiring the opposite-sex parent and wanting to eliminate the same-sex parent as a rival. Children resolve these conflicts by "identification with the aggressor," resolving guilt over unacceptable impulses by emulating same-sex parents. Understanding children's shift of focus from parents to friends when they start school (D) reflects Freud's Latency stage, when psychosexual impulses are buried to permit expanding social and academic experiences.

64. C: It is not a coincidence that children in Piaget's Concrete Operations stage of cognitive development are around elementary-school age. In this stage they are first able to perform mental operations with logical sequences when associated with concrete events, enabling them to learn basic arithmetic and conjugate verbs, etc. Toddlers (A) and preschoolers (B) are typically in Piaget's Preoperational stage and cannot yet think logically. Middle school-aged children (C), i.e. ages 11-14, typically progress from Piaget's stage of Concrete Operations into his Formal Operations stage, wherein they can perform logical mental operations abstractly, without concrete events.

65. C: In ECE settings, teachers and administrators should create organized outlines containing guidelines for developmentally appropriate practices and outcomes. These should include the schedules and methods for introducing and reinforcing the guidelines at each stage. Based on these outlines, educators can then use authentic assessments, observations, and other means of monitoring children's progress. Lesson plans should not only promote attainment of the developmental guidelines, but also appeal to children's interests (A) to be meaningful. Progress tracking should not only be systematic, but also follow developmental sequences (B). Progress monitoring reveals class and individual levels of performance to inform lesson planning and identify individual children needing added support. Children performing above group level should receive enrichment activities; those performing below group level should receive 1:1 support, rather than vice versa (D).

66. A: The Brigance Diagnostic Inventory of Early Development is a formal assessment designed for planning instruction with children aged 0–7 years. The Infant-Toddler Developmental Assessment (B) is a formal assessment designed to screen for developmental delays in children aged 0–42 months. The Bayley Scale for Infant Development (C) is a formal assessment designed for assessing developmental delays in children aged 1–42 months. The Early Coping Inventory (D) is a formal assessment designed for planning interventions with children aged 4–36 months.

67. C: The amount that a transparent medium slows down the speed of light through it is called the index of refraction. The normal line (A) is an imaginary line that runs at a right angle to the surface of a medium; in the example given, it would be the waterline in the glass of water. The wavelength (B) of the light becomes shorter in proportion to how much the speed of light is slowed by the medium (but the medium does not change the frequency of the light wave, which is a property of the light source). The angle of refraction (D) is the degree to which the light wave is bent by the medium. As an example of refraction indices, diamonds trap light and slow its speed more than water because they are much denser and harder than water; thus, they sparkle more than water does and have a higher index of refraction than water.

68. A: Through gills. Animals of the phylum Mollusca respire through gills. Respiration is the process of taking in oxygen and releasing carbon dioxide. Mollusks include five classes that include species as diverse as chitons, land and marine snails, and squid. This represents a diverse range of body structures. Many mollusks have a mantle that includes a cavity that is used for both breathing and excretion. Within the mantle are gills (ctenidia). Mollusks do not have tracheas. Some land snails have reduced gills that feature a respiratory cavity but are not true lungs. Muscle contraction is not required for ventilation of the gills. Other structures, such as cilia, work to pass water over the gills.

69. A: Liquids (C), gases (D), and plasma (B) are fluids. They share certain properties, e.g., not keeping any shape and spreading indefinitely outside of containers. Solids (A) are not fluids because they have specific atomic structures that are crystalline or three-dimensional, and specific melting points. Solids have the most cohesive molecules; gases have the least cohesive molecules; and liquids have molecules in between solids and gases in cohesion. Plasma is considered distinct from gas, due to the charges placed on the atoms, but it shares many of the properties of gases.

70. A: Tree. In the food chain of tree → caterpillar → frog → snake → hawk → worm, the tree is at the trophic level with the greatest amount of energy. Trophic level refers to the position of an organism in a food chain. Energy is lost according to the laws of thermodynamics as one moves up the food chain because it is converted to heat when consumers consume. Primary producers, such as autotrophs, are organisms who are at the base and capture solar energy. Primary consumers are herbivores that feed on the producers. Secondary consumers consume primary consumers and so on. Decomposers get their energy from the consumption of dead plants and animals.

71. D: Power = work / time. The mass of the object (10 kg) and the distance (10 m) can be used to calculate work. The value for time is also provided.

72. B: A spoiling apple. A spoiling apple is an example of a chemical change. During a chemical change, one substance is changed into another. Oxidation, a chemical change, occurs when an apple spoils. Sublimation of water refers to the conversion between the solid and the gaseous phases of matter, with no intermediate liquid stage. This is a phase change, not a chemical reaction. Dissolution of salt in water refers to a physical change since the salt and water can be separated again by evaporating the water, which is a physical change. Breaking a rock is an example of a physical change where the form has changed but not the substance itself.

73. C: Chemical sedimentary rocks are formed from deposits of minerals, as when flooding introduces water, which has minerals dissolved in it, and then the water evaporates, leaving behind layers of precipitated minerals no longer in solution without the water. Limestone is a chemical sedimentary rock, as are gypsum and rock salt. Clastic (A) sedimentary rock forms from clasts or little bits of rock that are compacted and cemented together. Organic (B) sedimentary rock forms from organic material like calcium from the bones and shells of animals. Pegmatite (D) is not a type of sedimentary rock; it is an intrusive igneous rock formed underground from cooling volcanic magma.

74. B: Gradualism states that evolution occurs slowly, with organisms exhibiting small changes over long periods of time. According to gradualism, the fossil record should show gradual changes over time. Punctuated equilibrium states that evolution occurs in spurts of sudden change. According to punctuated equilibrium, the fossil record should have large gaps. Therefore, the correct answer is choice B.

75. A: The reason the sky looks blue to us is because the earth's atmosphere absorbs the wavelengths of all colors of light in the spectrum except for the wavelengths of the color blue, which it reflects back so that we see it. Therefore (B) is incorrect. Glass appears transparent to us; however, it is really only transparent to the light frequencies (wavelengths) that we can see, but to ultraviolet light frequencies, which we cannot see, glass is actually opaque. Wood, metal, and other materials look opaque to us *not* because they reflect light (D), but rather because they absorb light.

76. D: When the electrons are strongly bound to the atoms of a substance, these atoms seldom release their electrons and thus do not conduct electricity well; such materials are electrical insulators—e.g., air, wood, glass, plastic, cotton, and ceramics. Metals and other substances whose atoms have free electrons that can separate from the atoms and move about are electrical conductors; electrical current flows freely through materials with loose electrons.

77. C: When children conduct simple experiments and are able to see patterns and meanings in the results, they are using the scientific process skill of inference. They use the skill of measurement (A) when they quantify the various physical properties of objects, like length, width, height, weight, etc. They use the skill of classification (B) when they group objects, events, conditions, or situations according to the properties they share in common. They use the skill of prediction (D) when they apply their experiences from experimenting to form new hypotheses to test.

78. B: When young children fit pegs into matching holes, or distribute one item to each child in their group, they are developing 1:1 correspondence concepts. When they see how many coins are in a piggy bank or how many children are in their group (A), they are developing counting concepts. When they divide objects into piles of the same type or shape (C), they are developing classification concepts. When they transfer sand, rice, water, or other substances from one container to others with different sizes and shapes (D), they are developing measurement concepts.

79. C: When building block structures and then dismantling them, children learn concepts of part-whole relations. They learn concepts of shape (A) when they realize that some objects roll away from them and others do not. They learn concepts of weight (B) when they try to lift different objects and find some are heavier and some lighter. As babies, they quickly learn concepts of temporal sequences (D) when they awaken wet and/or hungry and then their parents change and/or feed them. As toddlers, they also learn temporal concepts through playing, tiring, and sleeping.

80. A: Water vapor is a gas, i.e., the gaseous form of water, which is a liquid at standard temperatures and pressures.

81. D: Igneous rocks are formed when magma in Earth erupts through cracks in the crust where it cools creating a hard structure with many air pockets or holes.

82. B: Temperature is a measure of the kinetic energy of particles. As temperature increases the average kinetic energy also increases. As the gas particles move more rapidly they occupy a larger volume. The increase in speed of the individual particles combined with the greater distance over which any intermolecular forces must act results in a decrease in the intermolecular forces.

83. B: The first step in the scientific method is to ask a research question to which we want to find an answer. The second step is to formulate a hypothesis (A), which is an educated guess about the answer to the research question. The third step is to conduct an experiment (C) to test the hypothesis. The final steps are to decide whether the results of the experiment prove or disprove the hypothesis, and then to report this to others (D).

84. A: After approaching calmly, stopping any behaviors that cause physical or emotional harm (step 1), and acknowledging the children's feelings (step 2), the third step in this conflict-mediation/resolution process* is to accumulate as much information as is necessary about the particular conflict from the involved parties. The fourth step is for the mediator to reiterate or restate what the problem is (C). The fifth step is to ask the involved children to think of and suggest potential solutions to the problem identified, and then help them agree to one selected solution (B). The sixth step is to follow up the conflict resolution by providing the involved parties with whatever support they need (D). *[from the HighScope Educational Research Foundation]

85. C: According to family systems theory, boundaries pertain to what a family includes and excludes, its limits, and its relative levels of togetherness and separation. Characteristics of disengaged families include *less* restricted or closed boundaries rather than vice versa (A); valuing independence more highly than enmeshed families do rather than vice versa (B); and being more open to considering new input (C). Characteristics of enmeshed families include having more restricted or closed boundaries than disengaged families, rather than looser and more flexible ones (D), and valuing togetherness, belonging, and loyalty more than autonomy.

86. D: The first level of EC self-awareness is differentiation, wherein children realize their reflections in mirrors are making the same movements they are, and they can tell their mirror reflections apart from other people, showing differentiation of self. The second level is situation, wherein children understand that their mirror reflections are unique to the self, and that their selves, bodies, and other things are physically situated in space. The third level is identification, wherein children can identify their mirror reflections as "me." When they see a mark on their faces by looking at a mirror, they reach for their own faces rather than for the mirror image. The fourth level is permanence, wherein children realize a permanent self, recognizing themselves in photographs and videos despite their different ages, places, clothing, etc. in these records. The fifth level is self-consciousness, also called meta-self-awareness, wherein children can see the self from the perspectives of others as well as from their own.

87. C: Native American and Asian cultures tend to be collectivist; i.e., they value interdependence among people, relationships, and social interactions. Latin American and African cultures also are more likely to embrace collectivism, focusing on the common good more than individual achievement; thus (A) is incorrect. Individualism, however, is *more* common in Canadian and Australian cultures, not less; so (B) is incorrect. European and North American cultures also favor individual expression, self-determination, independence, uniqueness, and self-actualization; hence they are more individualistic cultures, not more collectivist, so (D) is incorrect.

88. C: In cartography, the scale of miles on a map enables us to estimate actual distances between places. For example, a map's scale of miles may state that one inch equals 500 miles. Thus, a ratio is required to interpret this information: by measuring with a ruler, if we see that the distance on the map between two cities, states, or countries equals six inches, then we can estimate the actual distance between these locations to be 3,000 miles. The key or legend (A) on a map identifies what the different symbols and colors used in the map indicate. The compass rose (B) on a map shows north, south, east, and west directions so we can see the orientations of different places. The lines in a grid (D) on a map indicate latitudes, or parallels, which run east-west, and longitudes, or meridians, which run north-south. By finding the intersection of latitude and longitude coordinates for a given place, we can determine its absolute location.

89. B: Baumrind designated Authoritative as the ideal parenting style for combining assertiveness and forgiveness; using discipline that is supportive rather than punitive; setting rules, but also explaining reasons for rules to children; being warm, nurturing, and responsive but also setting limits and boundaries; and democratically receiving, considering, and addressing children's viewpoints rather than ignoring them. Baumrind described the Authoritarian (A) style as directive, demanding, punitive, strict, and unresponsive. These parents make rules without explaining them and are not as warm or nurturing. She described the Uninvolved (C) style as one that makes neither demands nor responses. These parents meet children's basic needs, but are otherwise detached and uncommunicative. In the extreme, they can reject or neglect children. Permissive (D) parents are warm, nurturing, responsive, and communicative, but do not set rules and limits or discipline children.

90. C: One geographical concept is distance. For example, product prices are affected by the cost of transportation, which in turn is affected by how far away raw materials are from the factories that process them, and prices for land closer to highways are higher than for land farther away from them. Location is another geography concept. Absolute location is determined by a place's latitude and longitude, not land prices (A). Relative location is determined by a region's changing characteristics, which surrounding areas can influence; one example is that land costs more in urban than rural areas. Relative location is not determined by latitude and longitude (B). Achievability is related to the accessibility of a geographical area; for example, villages with surrounding forests or swamps are less accessible than those on beaches. The dependency of an area, and hence its achievability, *does* change (D) as its technology, transportation, and economy change.

91. A: Popular approaches to conflict resolution for early childhood ages (e.g., the HighScope program) are typically very similar in their steps to the steps used in adult conflict mediation. When adults intervene in a conflict among young children, they are advised to listen to children's feelings, and also to acknowledge these rather than not saying anything (B). Adults should not only gather information from the children about their conflict, but should also restate the problem identified by the children rather than not talking about it (C). Suggesting possible solutions is something an adult should ask the children to do themselves rather than doing it for them (D); the adult should then help the children come to an agreement about which solution they choose. Adults should follow up with support as needed.

92. B: In the early development of self-awareness, infants normally demonstrate eye-hand coordination by systematically reaching for and touching things they see by the age of 4 months (A). They regulate their reaching behaviors according to their physical sitting, posture, and balance levels by 4–6 months of age (C). They can typically tell the difference between video of themselves and of other babies dressed in identical clothing by the age of 6 months (D). They typically can tell the difference between live video of themselves and of others exactly mimicking their behaviors by the ages of 4–7 months (B).

93. B: Most infants typically develop the behavior of sharing activities with their peers, most notably activities involving toys or other concrete objects, by the age of one year. They have usually developed the motor and cognitive skills to walk and talk by the time they are two years old, enabling them to coordinate their behaviors while they play with their peers (A). From around three to five years old, children's development of the understanding of symbolic representation increases, as evidenced by their increasing engagement in "make-believe" scenarios (D) and pretend play. So, too, do their prosocial behaviors of helping and caring for others (C) increase during this early childhood period.

94. B: When a dominant culture absorbs other cultures so that they all adopt all the behaviors of the dominant culture, this is called assimilation: the dominant culture assimilates other cultures. When different ethnic groups unite to form a new culture, this is also assimilation, not acculturation

(A). The adoption by one culture of some of another culture's traits is acculturation, not assimilation (C). When two or more different cultures virtually fuse, this is also a type of acculturation rather than assimilation (D).

95. B: Permissive parents are nurturing, responsive, and communicative with their children. However, they avoid confronting and/or disciplining children and do not expect them to demonstrate much self-control or maturity. Consequently, their children tend to have problems with authority figures, poor school performance, and deficits in self-regulation. The children of unresponsive, overly strict, demanding, harshly punitive authoritarian (A) parents tend to develop proficient technical and school performance and obedience, but lack social skills, self-esteem, and happiness. The children of authoritative (C) parents, who have the ideal parenting style, tend to develop competence, success, and happiness. Uninvolved (D) parents, who are undemanding but also unresponsive, uncommunicative, and detached, and may even neglect or reject children, produce children lacking competence, self-esteem, and self-control.

96. D: Identification is the third of five progressive levels of self-awareness that children develop. In differentiation (B), the first level, children can distinguish their mirrored images from other people, and realize that their reflection's movements correspond to their own movements. In situation (C), the second level, children then realize their mirror images are unique to themselves and that their bodies and selves are situated in space. In identification (D), the third level, children identify their reflections as "me." When they see something on their reflected faces, they know to touch their faces rather than the mirror to touch or remove the object. In permanence (A), the fourth level, children realize their self is permanent over time and space, recognizing themselves in photos and videos regardless of their ages, clothing, location, etc. (The fifth level is self-consciousness or "meta"-self-awareness, i.e., seeing oneself from others' as well as one's own perspective.)

97. C: Babies typically develop the self-awareness ability to differentiate between live video of themselves and people imitating their behaviors around four to seven months of age. Newborns (A) demonstrate the self-awareness ability of differentiating their bodies from the environment and internal/self from external/other stimulation from birth. Two-year-olds (B) demonstrate awareness of symbolic representation, understanding that mirror images and photos represent themselves. Babies typically regularly reach for things they see around four months of age. Around four to six months (D) of age, babies are able to regulate their reaching movements according to their postural and balance levels.

98. A: Historically, slave owners did not permit the African slaves they bought to learn how to read and write. Though some slaves still managed secretly to attain literacy, the majority suffered forced illiteracy and thus developed a rich oral tradition of storytelling, songs, etc., which they transmitted to succeeding generations. Latin American culture has had a significant influence on North American music and dance (B), as evidenced in the growing popularity of Latino music within North American popular music, and in the Latin division of ballroom dancing. Recent Asian immigrants do not all immediately adopt American family structures (C); when arriving in America, extended families (grandparents, aunts, uncles, cousins, etc.) are more likely to continue living together. The policies of European-American settlers have eradicated much of Native Americans' tribal culture (D); while some groups have worked hard to preserve their tribal languages, religions, music, dance, artwork, and other customs, overall much of their culture has been lost along with much of their population.

99. A: The phenomenon of "sticky prices" refers to prices that stay the same even though it seems they should change (either increasing or decreasing).

100. A: The 10th Amendment establishes that any power not given to the federal government in the Constitution belongs to the states or the people. The federal and local governments share many responsibilities.

Practice Test #2

1. Among major congenital structural defects in newborns, which one is the most common in the USA?

    a. Spina bifida
    b. Cleft palates
    c. Heart defects
    d. Clubbed feet

2. Which of these most accurately reflects expert guidelines for early childhood nutrition?

    a. Give children drinks equally balancing water, milk, soda, and juices.
    b. Give children fruit juices instead of whole fruits to prevent choking.
    c. Give children whole milk until age 2, and skim or 1% milk thereafter.
    d. Give children more beef as a protein source superior to other foods.

3. In order to achieve _____, Piaget said children accomplish _____ and _____ as processes included in the larger process of _____.

    a. Adaptation; equilibrium; assimilation; accommodation
    b. Assimilation; accommodation; adaptation; equilibrium
    c. Equilibrium; assimilation; accommodation; adaptation
    d. Accommodation; assimilation; equilibrium; adaptation

4. According to Piaget's theory, which of these abilities develops earliest in children?

    a. Reversibility of actions
    b. Conservation of quantity
    c. Symbolic representation
    d. Object permanence

5. An adult pours the same amounts of liquid from two identically sized and shaped containers into a short, wide glass and a taller, thinner glass as a preschool child watches. The adult asks the child which glass holds more liquid. The child answers that the taller one must hold more, because the liquid in it comes up higher. This best illustrates which characteristic of preschoolers' thinking, according to Piaget's theory of cognitive development?

    a. Object permanence
    b. Decentration
    c. Reversibility
    d. Centration

6. During Piaget's Sensorimotor stage of cognitive development, which occurs last?

    a. Coordination of Reactions
    b. Tertiary Circular Reactions
    c. Secondary Circular Reactions
    d. Primary Circular Reactions

7. A schema is best defined as a(n):

    a. Motor behavior
    b. Intentional action
    c. Reflexive reaction
    d. Mental construct

8. For a culturally diverse preschool class, which is the best example of an instructional strategy to benefit all the children by validating their individual cultural backgrounds?

a. Using learning materials and activities to teach greetings in all the children's family languages
b. Incorporating the holidays observed by all of the children's cultures into the curriculum design
c. Supplying classroom materials about diverse countries, including those of all children's families
d. Directing the children they must accept and play for equal amounts of time with all classmates

9. What has research most often found about parental reading to infants when comparing ethnic groups and socioeconomic status?

a. Reading to infants differs more among ethnic groups than between poor or non-poor.
b. In each ethnic group studied, poor parents read less to infants than non-poor parents.
c. Parents tend to read to their infants the same amount regardless of their ethnic group.
d. Studies find that ethnicity determines how responsive parents are toward their infants.

10. What is true about the sleeping and waking cycles of babies?

a. Circadian rhythms are present in infants when they are born.
b. Circadian rhythms begin to develop around six weeks of age.
c. Circadian rhythms cause regular sleep cycles by two months.
d. Circadian rhythms are regulated by internal body processes.

11. Research finds which of the following to be responsible for the most birth defects in babies?

a. Genetic causes
b. Environmental causes
c. Combined genetic and environmental causes
d. Causes which are undetermined or unknown

12. Which statement is most accurate about ECE experts' approach to cultural influences?

a. Cultural sensitivity involves knowing culture equals ethnicity and ecological niche.
b. Cultural sensitivity involves cultural scripts others are aware of and can articulate.
c. Cultural sensitivity involves having comprehensive knowledge of others' customs.
d. Cultural sensitivity involves sincere efforts to understand beliefs and their effects.

13. An adult has two identically sized and shaped containers holding identical amounts of liquid. S/he pours the same amount from each container into a short, wide glass and a tall, thin glass as a seven-year-old watches. The adult asks the child which container holds more. The child answers, "They both hold the same amount; I just saw you pour the same amount into each glass." This child demonstrates which ability according to Piaget's theory of cognitive development?

a. Centration of property
b. Permanence of objects
c. Conservation of volume
d. Egocentrism of thought

14. In Piaget's theory of cognitive development, which stages occur during early childhood, i.e., from birth to the age of eight years?

   a. Sensorimotor, Preoperational, Concrete Operations
   b. Preoperational, Concrete Operations, Formal Operations
   c. Sensorimotor, Preoperational, Formal Operations
   d. None of these stages occur during early childhood.

15. Experts recommend including in ECE programs five factors to prevent child abuse and neglect. Two of these are to enhance parental (1) resilience and (2) social connections. Which of the following is NOT one of the other three?

   a. Strengthening child development and parenting knowledge
   b. Offering concrete help to families when they are needing it
   c. Strengthening children's emotional and social competence
   d. Strengthening legal punishment for child abuse and neglect

16. According to EC experts, which of these is most accurate regarding supporting young children's physical fitness?

   a. Adults should choose when and what to do, as young children cannot.
   b. Adults should give only verbal directions to promote language growth.
   c. Activities should permit every child's success, irrespective of skill level.
   d. Young children need to do a single familiar activity until they master it.

17. Which of the following actions represents the use of a fine motor skill?

   a. Reaching for a pen
   b. Picking up a crayon
   c. Sitting down on a chair
   d. Standing up from a seat

18. Researchers find that how many babies are born annually in America with some major birth defect?

   a. About 1%
   b. About 5%
   c. About 2%
   d. About 3%

19. Recent research into early sibling relationships has most found which of these?

   a. Age and gender differences greatly influence sibling relations.
   b. Parents are better role models than siblings for all social skills.
   c. When children have older siblings they will turn out like them.
   d. Positive sibling relationships teach important social behaviors.

20. Which of the following did Piaget say children develop at the oldest ages?

   a. Magical thinking
   b. Symbolic thinking
   c. Intuitive thinking
   d. Deductive logic

21. What is a correct conclusion showing internal consistency in instruments used to test preschoolers?

    a. Different questions, tasks, and stimuli within one instrument all measure aspects of the same construct.

    b. In a comprehensive test of multiple developmental domains, all of the subscale scores should correlate.

    c. In a comprehensive test of multiple domains, the scores for subscales correlate with the full-scale score.

    d. Children with different developmental needs make similar scores from different items on the same test.

22. What is recommended for ECE facilities to do regarding existing custody arrangements of the children they serve?

    a. ECE program administrators can make decisions regarding the legal and/or physical custody of children they serve.

    b. ECE staff should request, and closely inspect, photo identification of anyone they do not recognize picking up a child.

    c. ECE programs should know enrolled children's custody status; but getting signed, dated documents is of no benefit.

    d. Parents enrolling children in ECE programs are not asked to list emergency contact information for any other adults.

23. What statement is most accurate about medical emergencies and treatment in ECE settings?

    a. ECE staff should always call an ambulance in all emergencies rather than requesting transportation from parents.

    b. ECE administrators must designate vehicles and employees for transport when awaiting ambulances is impossible.

    c. ECE administrators should recruit as many staff members as possible to help with medical emergency treatments.

    d. ECE staff administrators designate for assistance in emergencies do not necessarily need current first aid training.

24. Among the following, which is true for EC teachers to establish and maintain good communication with parents?

    a. When an EC teacher calls each parent during the first two weeks of school, it causes alarm for most parents.

    b. It is easier for teachers to call parents later in the school year if issues warrant if they did not first call earlier.

    c. Parents learn to expect no communication if teachers publish print/online weekly/monthly class newsletters.

    d. Parents perceive teachers sending home parent letters at the beginning of the school year as more available.

25. Among the following, which is correct regarding the legal responsibilities of ECE centers if enrolled children are not picked up on time by parents or other authorized adults.

a. Once the center's hours are over, it is no longer legally responsible for the welfare of any child on its premises.
b. ECE staff members are less likely to incur legal liability if they keep the child at their home than at the ECE center.
c. If ECE staff must remove a child from the center, they must inform the police of where they are taking the child.
d. If parents are frequently late picking up children, ECE staff must contact authorities rather than question parents.

26. Which of these is included among things educators can do to involve diverse families in EC education?

a. If parents cannot attend meetings due to work, educators cannot help it.
b. It is outside educator responsibility to provide transportation or childcare.
c. School strategies are in educators' purviews, but not home-use strategies.
d. Educators can recruit interested family members to help out at preschool.

27. Which of the following applies to concurrent validity of screening and assessment instruments used with EC populations?

a. The authors of a new intelligence test have confidence in its statistical strength rather than comparison.
b. The authors of a new intelligence test have compared its results with the Stanford-Binet and the WPPSI.
c. EC educators have a new intelligence test with very different results than Stanford-Binet or than WPPSI.
d. EC educators have a new intelligence test and cannot compare it to tests with prior established validity.

28. What statement accurately represents norm-referenced or criterion-referenced tests and/or how they are applied in screening and assessing EC populations?

a. A criterion-referenced test determines how similar a child's performance is to the average for that age level.
b. A norm-referenced test determines how a child's results compare to performance standards for grade level.
c. A criterion-referenced test measures how well a certain child has mastered various developmental domains.
d. A criterion-referenced test can identify children who are performing significantly above and below averages.

29. What is true regarding EC education relative to young children's families and communities?

a. Educators should design and plan curriculum and instruction on their own.
b. Educators are responsible to plan instruction without community resources.
c. Educators should protect children's education by containing it in the school.
d. Collaborating with communities strengthens schools, families, and learning.

30. Which of these is true regarding guidelines for ECE programs related to children's non-emergency medical illnesses, chronic conditions, and possible emergencies?

a. When a child gets sick, the parents rather than ECE staff decide if the child should leave an ECE facility.
b. Non-emergency medical treatments do not require filed procedures and reports like emergencies do.
c. Doctors and nurses are not authorized to provide routine medical treatment by parent consent forms.
d. Information on chronic medical conditions and treatment directions should be on file, but not posted.

31. Which of these is accurate regarding individual observations a teacher could make for informal assessments of students in pre-K classes?

a. Teachers would not use a checklist to conduct individual informal assessments.
b. Teachers might keep running records, but should not utilize anecdotal records.
c. Teachers cannot assemble portfolio assessments of children's work for these.
d. Teachers can fill out a chart of various domains with child strengths and needs.

32. Which of these reflects valid applications of screening and/or assessment instruments in ECE programs?

a. Evaluating children's achievement of program goal-related learning outcomes is an inappropriate use.
b. Children's progress and changes over time should be monitored using other tools than assessments.
c. Teacher effectiveness for furthering children's achievement of learning outcomes can be evaluated.
d. EC educators never apply the results of assessments in planning curriculum or treatment programs.

33. Which of these is characteristic of DR-TA approaches, but not of DRA approaches, to using basal readers for teaching reading?

a. Questions that require convergent thinking
b. Specifications for when to teach which skills
c. Application is limited more to basal readers
d. No pre-instruction for new vocabulary words

34. Which of the following is true about instructional strategies used in the basal reader approach to teaching reading, and/or about changes in basal readers from the past to the current century?

a. 20th-century basal reader series emphasized comprehension over control of vocabulary.
b. Skills acquisition is more important in current basal readers than enjoyment of reading.
c. Methods are more varied in 21st-century basal reader series than in 20th-century series.
d. Older basal reader series used more multiple versions of stories than current series do.

35. Which statement is most accurate regarding the whole language approach to literacy instruction in early childhood?

a. This approach does not emphasize giving children opportunities for independent reading.
b. This approach excludes activities that involve guided reading with small groups of children.
c. This approach believes children both learn to read by writing, and learn to write by reading.
d. This approach emphasizes early grammar, spelling, and other technical aspects are correct.

36. What statement is correct about the basal reader approach to reading instruction in early childhood?

    a. Several other approaches are commoner in the US than basal readers.
    b. The majority of USA's elementary school classrooms use basal readers.
    c. More publishers offer basal readers now than during the 20th century.
    d. Teachers are more responsible to explore readers for district approval.

37. Which of the following is NOT one of the steps for implementation of the Language Experience Approach (LEA) with young children?

    a. The teacher assigns a topic for teacher-guided discussion by the children.
    b. The children and teacher collaborate in choosing a topic to be discussed.
    c. Each child gets a turn saying his/her own sentence to advance the topic.
    d. Teachers record children's sentences and read records aloud frequently.

38. What is most accurate regarding the basal reader series used in today's classrooms?

    a. Texts used are by subjects, not reading levels.
    b. Texts used are expository, not narrative work.
    c. Texts used are the children's literature genre.
    d. Texts used are thematically organized by unit.

39. Which of the following statements is most accurate regarding inter-rater reliability of a screening or assessment instrument used in ECE settings?

    a. With tests using unstructured interviews, structured tasks, or observations, rater differences are normal.
    b. The test is unreliable if one rater scores a child with possible developmental delay and another as normal.
    c. When different assessors observe a child at different times or settings, different results show unreliability.
    d. Inter-rater reliability means an instrument measures different constructs depending on the administrator.

40. Third-grade students typically receive their spelling word lists each Monday so that they can practice them at home before the test on Friday. While their teacher is pleased that the students usually receive high grades on spelling tests she observes that they misspell those same words when writing in journals or doing classwork. How should this teacher modify her instruction?

    a. Post a list of vocabulary words when the students are writing to help them recall correct spellings.
    b. Integrate spelling words into writing, reading, grammar, phonics, and other activities to help students learn the words in a variety of contexts.
    c. Provide more time, such as a two-week period, between tests so that students have more time to study.
    d. Review the words before certain activities to increase immediate recall of correct spellings.

41. Which of the following is true about formal and informal observational screening and assessment instruments used with EC populations?

    a. Formal observations involve watching the child's activities in natural settings.
    b. Informal observations entail watching activities structured for the instrument.
    c. Observations include developmentally normal behaviors but not problem ones.
    d. Observations include description and evaluation of a child's social interactions.

42. Which of the following best explains the importance prior knowledge brings to the act of reading?

a. Prior knowledge is information the student gets through researching a topic prior to reading the text. A student who is well-prepared through such research is better able to decode a text and retain its meaning.

b. Prior knowledge is knowledge the student brings from previous life or learning experiences to the act of reading. It is not possible for a student to fully comprehend new knowledge without first integrating it with prior knowledge.

c. Prior knowledge is predictive. It motivates the student to look for contextual clues in the reading and predict what is likely to happen next.

d. Prior knowledge is not important to any degree to the act of reading because every text is self-contained and therefore seamless. Prior knowledge is irrelevant in this application.

43. Of the following, which statement is true about instruction in the alphabetic principle?

a. Letter-sound relationships with the highest utility should be the earliest ones introduced.

b. The instruction of letter-sound correspondences should always be done in word context.

c. Letter-sound relationship practice times should only be assigned apart from other lessons.

d. Letter-sound relationship practice should focus on new relationships, not go over old ones.

44. Regarding the age ranges addressed in different screening and assessment instruments that ECE programs use, which of these is correct?

a. Screening and assessment instruments typically cover wide ranges, such as from 2 to 16 years.

b. Screening and assessment instruments typically target specific age ranges, such as 0 to 36 months.

c. When a screening or assessment instrument covers a wide range, it is typically not subdivided.

d. The dynamic, rapid development of early childhood demands test instruments with sensitivity.

45. Which of the following is correct regarding the Directed Reading Activity (DRA) practice of reading instruction using basal readers?

a. DRA focuses on reading and writing rather than art, music, or drama.

b. Students read text aloud during the DRA but do not also read silently.

c. Teachers save new vocabulary/concepts until after students' reading.

d. Workbook / practice activities review comprehension and vocabulary.

46. Of the three tiers of words, the most important words for direct instruction are:

a. Tier-one words

b. Common words

c. Tier-two words

d. Words with Latin roots

47. What is most typical of the scoring and interpretation of preschool IQ scales and similar standardized tests?

a. Adding up points for each item response for a total score

b. Adding up values within sections to get a group of scores

c. Weighting item values, score conversion, and norm tables

d. Noting if a score surpasses a cut-off value for assessment

48. Which student is most likely to need referral to a reading specialist for assessment, special instruction, or intervention?

a. Annabel: a 2nd-grade student who tends to skip over words or phrases when she reads, affecting her comprehension of the text
b. Cliff: a kindergarten student who is already reading simple chapter books with his parents at home or in class
c. Noelle: a 1st-grader who avoids any activity in which she must read, both aloud and silently, preferring to ask an adult to read the text for her first
d. Barrett: a 3rd-grader who often confuses the sounds of certain letters, such as /b/ and /d/ or /v/ and /u

49. *Caret, carrot, to, two* and *too* share something in common. They:

a. Are nouns
b. Are monosyllabic
c. Are homophones
d. Are dipthongs

50. Of the following, which is/are NOT an example(s) of math manipulatives?

a. Tangrams for shape recognition
b. Large magnetic number boards
c. Printed mathematical formulas
d. Play money, toy cash registers

51. Which statement accurately reflects the philosophy and/or practice of the Bank Street Developmental Interaction Approach to early childhood education?

a. The behaviors of the individual teacher are more significant than classroom design.
b. Growing up in controlled environments enables children to develop self-discipline.
c. Different activities have strong, discrete boundaries so transitions are unnecessary.
d. Subjects of learning are changed at irregular intervals of time to promote flexibility.

52. The MLA guidelines for citing multiple authors of the same source in the in-text citations of a research paper are to use the first author's name and "et al" for the other(s) in the case of...

a. More than one author.
b. Two or three authors.
c. Three or more authors.
d. Four or more authors.

53. A child in kindergarten is *most* likely to be referred to a speech-language pathologist if s/he does not correctly produce which of the following phonemes?

a. /p/ as in pepper or poppies
b. /ʒ/ as in mirage or measure
c. /v/ as in velvet, valve, value
d. /s/ as in see, yes, or asking

54. Which of the following is accurate regarding Friedrich Froebel's philosophy and theory of education relative to early childhood?

    a. Froebel thought higher-order cognitive skills develop via verbal and numerical activities, not art.
    b. Froebel found virtues were taught via academic disciplines rather than through children's games.
    c. Froebel believed that the relationships between teachers and their students should be egalitarian.
    d. Froebel recommended authoritarian roles for teachers and limited roles for families in education.

55. Which of these does NOT correctly describe the learning activities of Early Childhood-aged students in one of the five areas included in Montessori Method schools?

    a. In the Cultural Subjects area, children learn how to converse in several different languages.
    b. In the Math and Geometry area, children count, do arithmetic, and use the decimal system.
    c. In the Language Arts area, children learn letter shapes, phonics, and oral verbal expression.
    d. In the Sensorial area, children sort/order/match colors, sounds, textures, smells, and tastes.

56. A teacher is working with a group of third graders at the same reading level. Her goal is to improve reading fluency. She asks each child in turn to read a page from a book about mammal young. She asks the children to read with expression. She also reminds them they don't need to stop between each word; they should read as quickly as they comfortably can. She cautions them, however, not to read so quickly that they leave out or misread a word. The teacher knows the components of reading fluency are:

    a. Speed, drama, and comprehension
    b. Cohesion, rate, and prosody
    c. Understanding, rate, and prosody
    d. Rate, accuracy, and prosody

57. Of the following statements, which adheres to Information Literacy standards?

    a. Students accessing information must critically evaluate it and its sources before using it.
    b. Students accessing information can ascertain how much of it they need after they find it.
    c. Students accessing information efficiently sacrifice broader scope and incidental learning.
    d. Students accessing information ethically must eschew using it to attain specific purposes.

58. What is a mnemonic device?

    a. A saying or image used to help remember a complex concept
    b. A tool that increases physical relaxation during a test
    c. An old-fashioned torture device involving repeated testing
    d. A tool for selecting answers on tests

59. The Scholastic Early Childhood Inventory (SECI), a formal assessment instrument, tests children's progress in domains that predict kindergarten readiness. Which of the following is NOT one of these domains?

    a. Mathematics
    b. Alphabet knowledge
    c. Scientific knowledge
    d. Phonological awareness

60. What should EC program administrators look for in screening and assessment instruments?

  a. Test instruments should measure developmental areas related to their programs.
  b. It is irrelevant whether a test instrument supports the goals set by the EC program.
  c. Staff skills are unrelated to test administration, scoring, and interpretation methods.
  d. Administrators should not be concerned with a test's statistical validity and reliability.

61. With a teacher's guidance, a class brainstorms main ideas, topics, or concepts from a text. Students choose a select number of these ideas and copy them onto separate index cards. The students then individually review the text, recording any supporting evidence on the notecard with the applicable main idea. This activity would be an excellent pre-lesson for teaching which skill set?

  a. Working as a group to interpret a text and write an appropriate and realistic sequel, focusing on interpretive comprehension and creative writing.
  b. Silent reading as a form of comprehension practice.
  c. Organizing ideas for writing a cohesive and persuasive essay or research paper that asserts supported arguments with valid supporting evidence.
  d. Literal and figurative comprehension, as well as contributing to group discussions via oral communication skills.

62. Regarding choices among available assessment instruments, which of these is accurate regarding how different EC programs should use their program goals to inform their selections?

  a. Outreach programs to identify untreated/undetected mental health disorders should pick tests of temperament.
  b. Programs such as Head Start for promoting general EC development should choose comprehensive assessments.
  c. Clinics specializing in treating children with regulatory disorders need social-emotional development assessments.
  d. Prevention programs helping multi-need families access supports and services should use several tests combined.

63. Research has found which of the following outcomes occur for students via revision and rewriting?

  a. Students only correct their mechanical errors in revisions.
  b. Students often incorporate new ideas when they rewrite.
  c. Students retain their original writing goals during revision.
  d. Students' planning in prewriting is unaffected in rewriting.

64. Whole language instruction in early childhood:

  a. Is implemented without regard for cultural diversity.
  b. Works to help children create meaning from reading.
  c. Does not aid children in expressing written meaning.
  d. Embraces all reading materials, regardless of quality.

65. Research into behavioral techniques has shown that which of these is the most powerful?

  a. Negative reinforcement
  b. Positive reinforcement
  c. Positive punishment
  d. Negative punishment

66. Which of the following statements correctly reflects one of the principles of emergent literacy theory?

    a. When young children "reread" storybooks, this means they have memorized them.
    b. Young children's invented spellings afford no information about phonetic familiarity.
    c. It is crucial for adults to read to young children, but not before they are a certain age.
    d. Reading and writing development are viewed as processes having successive stages.

67. What type of compound is formed by the combination of two or more non-metallic elements with one another?

    a. Organic
    b. Ionic
    c. Covalent
    d. Chemical

68. Which of the following observations provides the best evidence that sound can travel through solid objects?

    a. Sound waves cannot travel through a vacuum.
    b. The atoms of a solid are packed tightly together.
    c. If you knock on a solid object, it makes a sound.
    d. You can hear a sound on the other side of a solid wall.

69. Which action will help dissolve a gas in a liquid if the gas and liquid are placed in a sealed container?

    a. Heat the liquid.
    b. Cool the liquid.
    c. Shake the container.
    d. Decrease the pressure on the lid.

70. Which of the following is an example of chemical weathering?

    a. Rain freezing on the roadway
    b. Ivy growing on the side of a wooden house
    c. Vinegar fizzing when poured on a rock
    d. A river carrying sediment downstream

71. Which of the following is never true of a chemical reaction?

    a. Matter is neither gained nor lost.
    b. Heat is absorbed or released.
    c. The rate of the reaction increases with temperature.
    d. There are a different number of atoms for the products and the reactants.

72. The distance from the Earth to the Sun is equal to one:

    a. Astronomical unit.
    b. Lightyear.
    c. Parsec.
    d. Arcsecond.

73. Fossils are least likely to be found in

a. sedimentary rock.
b. metamorphic rock.
c. igneous rock.
d. Fossils are commonly found in all types of rock.

74. In a parallel circuit, there are three paths: A, B and C. Path A has a resistance of 10 ohms, path B a resistance of 5 ohms and part C a resistance of 2 ohms. How do the voltage and current change for each path?

a. Voltage and current are kept the same in each path.
b. Voltage is greatest in path A and current is greatest in path C.
c. Voltage is lowest in path C and current is greatest in path C.
d. Voltage is the same for each path and current is greatest in path C.

75. What happens to the temperature of a substance as it is changing phase from a liquid to a solid?

a. Its temperature increases due to the absorption of latent heat.
b. Its temperature decreases due to the heat of vaporization.
c. Its temperature decreases due to the latent heat of fusion.
d. Its temperature remains the same due to the latent heat of fusion.

76. Which of the following is an example of a descriptive study?

a. correlational studies of populations
b. identifying a control
c. statistical data analysis
d. identifying dependent and independent variables

77. Tropical climate zones are characterized by:

a. Extreme temperature variations between night and day.
b. Extreme temperature variations between seasons.
c. Frequent rainfall.
d. Relatively constant, cold temperatures (35°F - 45°F)

78. Once a hypothesis has been verified and accepted, it becomes a _____.

a. fact
b. law
c. conclusion
d. theory

79. Which of the following statements correctly compares rocks and minerals?

a. Minerals may contain traces of organic compounds, while rocks do not.
b. Rocks are classified by their formation and the minerals they contain, while minerals are classified by their chemical composition and physical properties.
c. Both rocks and minerals can be polymorphs.
d. Both rocks and minerals may contain mineraloids.

80. The process whereby a radioactive element releases energy slowly over a long period of time to lower its energy and become more stable is best described as _____.

  a. combustion
  b. fission
  c. fusion
  d. decay

81. The asteroid belt in our solar system is located between:

  a. Earth and Mars.
  b. Neptune and Pluto.
  c. Uranus and Saturn.
  d. Mars and Jupiter.

82. How does the tilt of Earth's axis cause seasons?

  a. A hemisphere experiences fall and winter when that half of Earth is tilted away from the Sun. It experiences spring and summer when that half of Earth is tilted towards the Sun
  b. A hemisphere experiences winter and spring when that half of Earth is tilted away from the Sun. It experiences summer and fall when that half of Earth is tilted towards the Sun
  c. A hemisphere experiences spring and summer when that half of Earth is tilted away from the Sun. It experiences fall and winter when that half of Earth is tilted towards the Sun
  d. A hemisphere experiences summer and fall when that half of Earth is tilted away from the Sun. It experiences winter and spring when that half of Earth is tilted towards the Sun

83. On a topographic map, an area where the contour lines are very close together indicates that

  a. a stream is present.
  b. the slope is very gentle.
  c. the slope is very steep.
  d. the area surrounds a depression.

84. According to research into differences among culturally diverse parents in America's age expectations for EC developmental milestones, which of the following is correct?

  a. Assessment data are no more likely to be misinterpreted when educators and parents have different rather than the same cultures.
  b. Due to cultural variations in when children achieve milestones, educators need not worry about developmental assessments.
  c. What parents from one culture view as developmentally normal can indicate developmental delay to parents from another culture.
  d. Regardless of parental cultural background, not reaching a developmental milestone by a certain age is always a cause for concern.

85. Which statement is most accurate regarding how educators in America can work with parents who are immigrants to this country?

a. Where parents and educators disagree on educational goals, educators must convince these parents to agree with them.
b. When children have developmental/learning problems, parents may need educators to inform them of available services.
c. When parents from other cultures do not advocate for their children to get needed services, this is due to a lack of interest.
d. When immigrant parents do not advocate for their children to get needed services, they are resisting confronting problems.

86. The Tropic of Capricorn:

a. separates the northern and southern hemispheres.
b. separates the eastern and western hemispheres.
c. is the southernmost latitude at which the sun can appear directly overhead at noon.
d. is the northernmost latitude at which the sun can appear directly overhead at noon.

87. Which of the following were dispatch riders notifying Americans of British troop movements reported by American surveillance in 1775?

a. Paul Revere and John Parker
b. William Dawes and Paul Revere
c. Andrew Johnson and William Dawes
d. John Parker and Phillip Dumay

88. Which of the following are more appreciated by individualistic cultures than by collectivist cultures?

a. Socially and relationally oriented behaviors
b. Working together for the good of the group
c. Interdependence rather than independence
d. Scientific thinking and manipulation of objects

89. Most federal judges have served as local judges, lawyers, and law professors. These are _____ qualifications.

a. Formal
b. Required
c. Informal
d. Recommended

90. Regarding cultural influences on parental childcare and education preferences, which result is true?

a. Hispanic families in the U.S. are found to use preschool centers more.
b. Hispanic families in the U.S. are found to prefer home/family settings.
c. Caucasian and Hispanic families in the U.S. use center and home care equally.
d. Caucasian families in the U.S. are likely to prefer family/home settings.

91. The physical geography of a region most directly affects:

  a. The religious beliefs of the native population.
  b. The family structure of the native population.
  c. The dietary preferences of the native population.
  d. The language spoken by the native population

92. The Seven Years War, called the French and Indian War by the Colonists:

  a. Was the precursor to the American Revolution
  b. Was a conflict related to European colonization
  c. Primarily took place in Canada
  d. Ended European conquests

93. Which of the following statements is *not* an accurate statement about the Puritans in England?

  a. The Puritans unconditionally gave all their support to the English Reformation
  b. The Puritans saw the Church of England as too much like the Catholic Church
  c. The Puritans became a chief political power because of the English Civil War
  d. The Puritans' clergy mainly departed from the Church of England after 1662

94. Which part of a hurricane features the strongest winds and greatest rainfall?

  a. Eye wall
  b. Front
  c. Eye
  d. Outward spiral

95. According to family systems theory, which family system component reflects the family's physical and emotional environment and its emotional quality?

  a. Hierarchy
  b. Boundaries
  c. Climate
  d. Equilibrium

96. In geography, which of the following is the best example of the concept of area differentiation?

  a. Fishermen find more use in the ocean than farmers; naturalists use forests more than academics.
  b. A region where farming is the main pursuit is rural; one where manufacturing dominates is urban.
  c. Land that is settled first or most frequently is often near natural resources like water, forests, etc.
  d. In one village, the predominant occupation is farming; in another village, fishing is more prevalent.

97. Which of the following best describes the significance of the U.S. Supreme Court's decision in the Dred Scott case?

  a. The ruling effectively declared slavery to be a violation of the Constitution.
  b. The ruling guaranteed full citizenship rights to freed slaves.
  c. The ruling turned many Southerners against the Supreme Court.
  d. The ruling furthered the gap between North and South and hastened the Civil War.

51

98. The Mason-Dixon Line divided:

    a. The East from the West before the western states were incorporated
    b. The East from the West along the Mississippi River
    c. The North from the South before the Civil War
    d. The Senate from the House of Representatives

99. The philosophy of the late 17th-18th centuries that influenced the Constitution was from the Age of:

    a. Enlightenment
    b. Empire
    c. Discovery
    d. Industry

100. Which geographic features were most conducive to the development of early civilizations?

    a. Rivers
    b. Deserts
    c. Forests
    d. Mountains

Answer Key and Explanations #2

1. C: 1 of every 150 infants in the USA is born with a heart defect, making this the most common major congenital structural defect in this country. Spina bifida (A), in which the spinal column/neural tube does not fuse completely; cleft palate (B), in which the palate and/or upper lip does not fuse completely; and clubbed feet (D), in which one or both feet is/are turned inward from the ankle, are also common congenital structural defects, but none is as common in the United States as heart defects are.

2. C: The Institute of Medicine, the American Academy of Pediatrics, the National Resource Center for Health and Safety in Child Care and Early Education, the Harvard School of Public Health and others recommend that parents and child care providers give children pasteurized whole milk until they are 2 years old and give children over the age of 2 years pasteurized skim or 1% fat milk. Experts advise adults to give young children safe water to drink as well as milk, but to avoid sodas and other sweetened drinks, and to limit juice to 4–6 ounces of 100% juice without added sweeteners daily (A). They recommend serving young children whole fruits instead of fruit juices (B). Leaner protein sources like poultry, beans, legumes, and low-fat yogurt/cottage cheese are recommended rather than beef (D), which should be limited due to its higher fat content. These guidelines are for both providing needed nutrients and preventing obesity.

3. C: In order to achieve equilibrium, or balance, Piaget said children accomplish assimilation, i.e. fitting new experiences into existing schemata; and accommodation, i.e. changing existing schemata or forming new ones in response to new experiences, as part of the larger process of adaptation, i.e. adjusting to the environment through interacting with it.

4. D: Object permanence, i.e. the understanding that things still exist when out of sight, develops in babies during Piaget's first, sensorimotor stage of cognitive development. Piaget believed the typical age for this development was around 8-9 months old. Some researchers after Piaget have also found evidence that some babies develop object permanence as young as 3 months old. Reversibility of actions (A) and conservation of quantity (C) develop during the stage of concrete operations, around the ages of 7-11 years. Symbolic representation (D) typically develops in the Early Representational Thought substage near the end of the Sensorimotor stage, around the ages of 18-24 months.

5. D: The child's focusing attention on only one property, i.e. height but not width, illustrates what Piaget termed centration. The inability to incorporate multiple properties makes the young child unable to conserve the quantity of liquid regardless of the container shape. Object permanence (A) is the realization that babies develop that things still exist when out of their view. Decentration (B) develops when older children no longer centrate on one property, but realize the taller glass is also thinner. Reversibility (C) develops around the same time, during Concrete Operations, when children can mentally reverse actions.

6. B: The order of the substages of Piaget's Sensorimotor stage are: Primary Circular Reactions (D); Secondary Circular Reactions (C); Coordination of Reactions (A); and Tertiary Circular Reactions (B). According to Piaget's original theory, while the beginning/ending ages of each stage can vary somewhat among individuals, the order of these stages does not vary.

7. D: Piaget coined the term schema to define a mental construct we form to categorize various classes/groups of things we encounter in the environment. Motor behaviors (A) are defined by Piaget as part of the first, Sensorimotor stage of cognitive development, when infants respond to

53

sensory stimuli with motor reactions. Babies begin to demonstrate intentional actions (B), i.e. purposeful behaviors, during the Sensorimotor substage called Coordination of Secondary Circular Reactions, when they realize the cause-and-effect relationships between their own actions and environmental responses. Reflexive reactions (C) or reflexes, like rooting, sucking, grasping, orienting to sounds, and vocalizing, are the earliest substage of the Sensorimotor stage infants undergo, from birth to 1 month old.

8. A: Young children develop cultural identities based on their family's cultural practices. Therefore, the preschool teacher can best address the cultural diversity of the class to benefit all students by giving them materials and activities wherein they all learn greetings in the languages of all their classmates, validating the cultural backgrounds of all children in the group. Incorporating various cultural holidays into the curriculum (B) or using multicultural classroom materials (C) alone would be insufficient for this purpose. Directing preschool-aged children to play for equal amounts of time with all classmates (D) is not feasible, as it is not a kind of behavior that can be controlled.

9. B: In various research studies, when ethnic groups (e.g., European-American, African-American, and Latino) are compared, there are differences in how much parents read to their infants (C) (e.g., many studies find European-American parents read a lot more to their infants than African-American parents, who read a little more to their infants than Latino parents). However, these differences are outweighed by the differences between poor and non-poor parents across ethnic groups (A). In each group, poor parents are much less likely to own any children's books, and they read less to their infants than non-poor parents do (B). Researchers studying this topic usually find little or no difference among ethnic groups in how responsive parents are to their infants (D).

10. B: Circadian rhythms are the sleeping and waking cycles of living beings. Human newborns do not have these at birth (A); they begin to develop when babies are around six weeks old (B). The majority of infants have developed regular cycles of sleeping and waking by the time they are 3–6 months old, not 2 months (C). Circadian rhythms are not regulated by internal body processes (D), but by periods of light and dark, as originally provided by natural daytime sunlight and nighttime darkness.

11. D: The March of Dimes reports that approximately 60% of all birth defects are due to unknown causes. The remaining roughly 40% of birth defects found in newborns have causes that are divided among genetic defects (A); prenatal environmental influences (B) like an expectant mother's exposure to various infections, medications, and/or substances; and combined genetic and environmental factors (C), which can cause congenital heart defects, neural tube defects like spina bifida, and cleft palates and cleft lips.

12. D: Experts on ECE, such as ZERO TO THREE National Center for Infants, Toddlers, and Families, say that cultural sensitivity involves sincere efforts by EC educators, service providers, advocates, program designers, policymakers, and others to understand the cultural beliefs of other people and the roles these beliefs play in how people parent their children and their goals for them. Working to understand these things is more important than accruing exhaustive knowledge of diverse customs (C). Experts also note that while cultural scripts guide parental and caretaking behaviors, people are often unaware of them and cannot explain them (B), which only makes them even more powerful as behavioral motivators, as people accept them as reality without reflection or analysis. Experts additionally point out that ethnicity, geographic area, social class, time lived in America, and other data can identify a family's ecological niche, but these do not equal their culture (A), i.e., their beliefs, values, and customs. They warn that equating ethnicity or ecological niche with culture can result in stereotypes.

13. C: This child demonstrates conservation of (liquid) volume by knowing both containers hold the same amount regardless of their shapes or sizes. Centration of property (A) is what a younger child does in focusing on only one property at a time, e.g. either the height or width of the container but not both. Piaget said centration prevents conservation. Object permanence (B) is the realization babies develop that things still exist even when they cannot see them. Egocentrism (D) is characteristic of the thinking of children in the Preoperational stage, when they cannot see things from another person's perspective but only their own.

14. A: The Sensorimotor stage is from birth to roughly age 2; the Preoperational stage from roughly ages 2-7 years; and the Concrete Operations stage from roughly ages 7-11 years. Therefore, infants to eight-year-olds are typically in one of these stages. The Formal Operations stage {(B), (C)} is around the age of 11 years and older. Therefore, answers (D) is incorrect.

15. D: The Center for the Study of Social Policy has recommended an approach to strengthen families that uses five factors for preventing child abuse and neglect. In addition to strengthening parental resilience and social connections, these also include strengthening parents' knowledge about child development and parenting (A); giving concrete assistance to families when they need it (B); and strengthening children's emotional and social competence (C). Increasing legal punishment for child abuse and neglect (D) is NOT included in this approach.

16. C: According to Head Start, adults should let young children choose among activities and when to switch to others, not choose for them (A). Young children are capable of this. Adults can create several "play stations", e.g., throwing a ball at a target; throwing a ball into a floor hoop; rolling a ball at a target; jumping over boxes on the floor; and jumping through floor hoops. Adults should use not only words, but also physical demonstrations of physical activities (B) divided into steps. This clarifies the physical actions involved, and also helps children who learn more visually than verbally (this is not only a matter of learning modality; it is also common in early childhood to learn via visual observation when language skills are less developed). Adults should provide open-ended and simple activities so children of any skill level can succeed (C). Young children's short attention spans mean they should be given frequent changes and variety in activities (D).

17. B: Fine motor skills involve small movements and small muscles, such as of the fingers, wrists, tongue, lips, and toes. An example is picking up a small object like a crayon or a spoon. Gross motor skills involve large movements and large muscles, as of the torso, arms, legs, and feet. Examples include rolling over and crawling, as infant developmental milestones; reaching for something (A) with the arms; sitting down (C); standing up (D); and running, jumping, climbing, kicking, throwing, catching, etc.

18. D: The American College of Obstetricians and Gynecologists (ACOG) finds that 3 of every 100 babies are born each year in America with some type of major birth defect. This equates to about 3%, which is more than (A) and (C) but less than (B). The March of Dimes says the number of babies born annually in America with birth defects is approximately 150,000.

19. D: Recent research has found that differences between sibling ages and genders have relatively little influence on sibling relationships (A). While parents are found to be better role models for social behaviors in more formal contexts, as in public or at dinner, older siblings are seen as better role models for social behaviors in more informal contexts, as with peers, in school, or on the streets (B). Research shows that while young children are influenced by older siblings, this does not necessarily mean they will turn out like them (C). Some make efforts to de-identify from siblings to avoid comparisons, which is another form sibling influence can take. Researchers find one of the most important things about early sibling relationships is the social behaviors and competencies children can learn from their siblings.

20. D: Deductive logic, i.e. applying general principles to predict specific instances, only develops fully during the stage of Formal Operations, around 11 years and older. Magical thinking (A) is typical of children in Piaget's Preoperational stage, from around 2-6 years. At this age their thinking is not logical but intuitive (C). Symbolic representation (B) develops near the end of the Sensorimotor stage, at ages around 18-24 months, when children begin to use objects to symbolize other objects during pretend/make-believe play. Inductive logic is the reciprocal concept to deductive logic. Instead of applying general principals to specific incidences, the thinker uses specific instances to draw generalizations. This type of thinking develops during the preoperational stage between ages around 2-6 years, earlier than deductive logic develops.

21. A: On a test designed to measure a particular construct, such as intelligence, even when a varied assortment of questions, tasks, and stimuli within the instrument measure different aspects, they should still all be aspects of the same construct for the test to have internal consistency. However, in comprehensive tests that cover multiple domains, one should not expect internal consistency among its subscales (B) that evaluate different domains of development, e.g. gross motor skills vs. language skills. Also, in such multi-domain tests, one should not expect internal consistency between each of the domains tested and the test's full-scale or overall score (C). But if children with different developmental needs receive similar scores on the same test through their responses to different test items (D), this is a sign that the test has low internal consistency.

22. B: Any time an adult whom the staff member(s) do(es) not recognize comes to pick up a child from an ECE facility, the staff should request photo identification of that person and closely inspect it. ECE program administrators are not legally authorized to make any decisions about the legal and/or physical custody of children their program serves (A). ECE program personnel should not just know every enrolled child's custody status; they should procure and keep on file a signed and dated document for each child indicating the child's custody status, names, contact information, and the relationships of all adults authorized to pick up the child (C), and copies of any separation agreements and/or court decisions. Parents enrolling children in ECE programs are always asked to list emergency contact information for other adults (D).

23. B: Administrators of ECE facilities must designate vehicles to use and employees responsible for transportation if an emergency is too serious to wait for an ambulance. However, when an emergency is non-life-threatening, staff should ask parents when available to transport their children (A). Administrators should keep the number of staff involved in emergency medical treatment to a minimum (C). The staff members designated by administrators to assist in medical emergencies should have current first aid training (D) and be willing to take the responsibility.

24. D: When ECE teachers send home letters to parents at the beginning of the school year, the parents perceive the teachers as more available and approachable. When an EC teacher calls each parent during the first two weeks of the school year, parents are more likely to appreciate and enjoy these conversations than to feel alarmed (A) by them. Calling parents early in the year also makes it easier to call them again later in the year if child issues warrant it (B). When ECE teachers publish a weekly or monthly class newsletter online, through e-mail, or in print, parents learn to expect communication from them (C).

25. C: If parents do not pick up a child at the end of the ECE center's day and do not notify the center why and/or when the child will be picked up for a long time, the center is still legally responsible for the child's welfare as long as the child is on its premises (A). ECE staff members are less likely to incur legal liability by keeping the child at the center than elsewhere, e.g. at their homes (B). If they must remove a child from the center, ECE staff should notify the police that they are moving the child and where they are taking the child (C). If parents are chronically late picking up children, ECE staff should inquire further of the parents (D) to find out why and work on possible solutions.

26. D: EC educators can involve diverse families in their children's educations by recruiting family members who express or show interest to help out at the preschool. If parents' work schedules prevent them from attending school meetings, proactive educators can adapt by scheduling the meetings at different times (A). Proactive educators can also provide transportation and childcare to facilitate parents' attendance to meetings and visits to the school (B). Educators can also involve diverse parents by sharing individualized strategies they can use at home with their children (B) that will support and extend the strategies used in school.

27. B: The Stanford-Binet Intelligence Scales and the WPPSI (Wechsler Preschool and Primary Scales of Intelligence) are both established instruments whose statistical validity and reliability have been proven. Since EC educators have confidence in these tests, a new instrument whose results compare closely to theirs would have high concurrent validity. Having confidence in a test's statistical strength, but without comparison to trusted existing tests, does not represent concurrent validity (A). If the new test gets very different results from established tests (C), this represents a lack of concurrent validity. If educators cannot compare a new test to existing tests for validity (D) or reliability, the new test is not shown to have concurrent validity.

28. C: Criterion-referenced tests measure the degree of a child's mastery of various developmental domains by comparing the child's performance against pre-established criteria or standards for performance. Norm-referenced tests determine how a child's performance compares to the *average* for his/her age (A) or grade level (B) rather than to pre-established criteria. *Norm*-referenced tests hence can identify children who are performing significantly above and below the averages (D) for their age or grade levels. A *criterion*-referenced test is better for monitoring changes over time in mastery levels. A norm-referenced test can monitor changes over time in performance relative to the average performance for the child's normative groups.

29. D: When educators collaborate with their communities, they realize benefits in stronger schools, families, and child learning. Educators should not just design and plan curriculum and instruction on their own (A), but should take advantage of all the community resources available to them (B) rather than keeping children's education isolated within the school (C).

30. A: If a child at an ECE facility develops a non-emergency illness, the staff must contact the parents, who will decide whether their child should leave the facility or not rather than the staff's deciding. Non-emergency medical treatments require ECE facilities to file procedures and reports the same as emergency treatments do (B). Parental consent forms should authorize doctors or nurses to provide routine medical treatment (C) of children who are in ECE facilities. Information on children's chronic medical conditions and directions for their treatment should not only be on file in ECE facilities, but should also always be posted for staff access (D).

31. D: One way teachers can use individual observations for informal assessments is to fill out a chart divided into domains like physical development, oral language development, math, emergent reading and writing, science, health, fine arts, technology and media, social studies, social-emotional development, and approaches to learning with one child's strengths and needs in each domain per chart. Another way is to complete a checklist (A). Another is to keep running records, and/or use anecdotal records (B) of children's progress. Teachers can also assemble portfolio assessments of children's work (C) as informal assessments of their learning over time.

32. C: One way that assessment instruments are used in ECE programs is to evaluate the children's achievement of the learning outcomes that define the program's goals (A); and by extension their teachers' effectiveness in furthering their achievement of those outcomes. Assessment tools are also applied to monitor children's progress and other changes over time (B). EC educators also use assessment results for planning curriculum and/or treatment programs (D).

33. D: Whereas DRA approaches include pre-teaching new vocabulary words to students before they read text that includes them, DR-TA approaches exclude any pre-instruction in favor of requiring students to engage in more the realistic activity of decoding new words as they read. Whereas DRA questions are mainly literal and factual, requiring only convergent thinking from students, DR-TA questions also demand divergent (creative) thinking by students (A), which stimulates higher levels of reader comprehension and interpretation. DRA manuals specify when to teach students which reading skills, while DR-TA approaches do not (B). DRAs are more limited to use with basal readers (C) due to their more specific directions, materials, and questions, while DR-TAs can be applied in other curriculum and lesson plans involving reading.

34. C: 21st-century basal reader series use a greater variety of methods in order to give children greater motivation for reading than were used in 20th-century and older series. 20th-century and older basal reader series emphasized vocabulary control (A) and skills acquisition (B) more than comprehension and enjoyment of reading, which are considered more important today. Compared to older series, current basal readers more often use multiple versions of stories (D) to afford students more choice and motivation in reading.

35. C: The whole language approach to early childhood literacy instruction does espouse the belief that learning reading and writing are each reciprocally active in helping children to learn the other. It does emphasize giving children many opportunities to read independently (A). It also includes activities involving guided reading with small groups of children (B). This approach does not emphasize children's early correctness with grammar, spelling, or other technical aspects of language (D), as children needing explicit instruction in decoding skills and strategies would have problems with them.

36. B: An estimated 75-85% of American classrooms use basal readers in grades K-8. This makes the basal reader the most common approach in America, more than any others (A). In the 21st century, far *fewer* publishers offer basal reader series than in the 20th. (C)—about ¼ as many as previously. This means teachers are *less* responsible for examining or piloting readers for district approval (D) than before.

37. A: In implementing the LEA with young children, the teacher does not assign a topic; rather, the children and teacher together agree on a choice of topic (B) the children will discuss with teacher guidance. Each child then has a turn saying his/her own sentence that advances the topic (C) of discussion. The teacher records each child's sentence verbatim without corrections, with this record visible to all children. Every few sentences, the teacher stops and reads this record aloud (D) and children confirm the record's accuracy.

38. D: Basal reader series feature texts that are graded by reading levels (A), include both expository and narrative writing (B), and in children's literature and various other writing genres (C) are thematically organized by unit (D).

39. B: If one rater of a test scores a child as possibly having a developmental delay or disorder, and another rater of the same test scores the same child as being within normal developmental limits, this means the test has poor inter-rater reliability and hence is unreliable for identifying the child's actual developmental status. Significant differences, especially with instruments using unstructured interviews, structured tasks, or observations, present problems and are not normal or expected (A). However, when different raters, such as teacher vs. parent, observe a child at different times and/or settings, like preschool vs. home, rater differences do NOT necessarily show unreliability (C) but are expected, because young children's behaviors can vary by settings and times. Inter-rater reliability means an instrument measures the *same* construct regardless of the administrator, not vice versa (D).

40. B: Spelling is often taught in a systematic way. Students receive words and memorize them for quizzes and tests. However, spelling is related to many aspects of language and must be treated as a dynamic subject. Integrating the words into other parts of language instruction will help students not only learn how to spell correctly, but also to recall meanings of words and various rules of English spelling and grammar. By using the same words in different subjects, the students will retain the information more readily than if they study the words intensely for one week in only one context.

41. D: The observations made of a child by trained observers using formal observational screening and assessment tools include descriptions and evaluations of the child's social interactions with others. They also can include developmentally normal behaviors the child demonstrates as well as problem behaviors the child demonstrates (C). Formal observations involve watching the child perform activities structured for the given instrument (A) while informal observations involve watching the child's activities in natural settings (B) like at home or in preschool during play times, not vice versa.

42. B: Prior knowledge is knowledge the student brings from previous life or learning experiences to the act of reading. It is not possible for a student to fully comprehend new knowledge without first integrating it with prior knowledge. Prior knowledge, which rises from experience and previous learning, provides a framework by which new knowledge gained from the act of reading can be integrated. Every act of reading enriches a student's well of prior knowledge and increases that student's future ability to comprehend more fully any new knowledge acquired through reading.

43. A: While there is no consensus among experts as to any universal sequence of instruction for teaching the alphabetic principle through phonics instruction, they do agree that, to enable children to start reading words as soon as possible, the highest-utility relationships should be introduced earliest. For example, the letters *m, a, p, t,* and *s* are all used frequently, whereas the *x* in *box*, the sound of *ey* in *they*, and the letter *a* when pronounced as it is in *want* have lower-utility letter-sound correspondences. Important considerations for the alphabetic principle are to teach letter-sound correspondences in isolation, not in word contexts (B); to teach them explicitly; to give students opportunities to practice letter-sound relationships within their other daily lessons, not only separately (C); and to include cumulative reviews of relationships taught earlier along with new ones in practice opportunities (D).

44. D: Early childhood is a period marked by dynamic, rapid developmental changes; hence the test instruments used must be sensitive to such changes. Some instruments cover wide ranges, like 2-16 years (A) while others target much more specific ranges like 0-36 months (B). When a test covers a wide age range, it may be subdivided into sections (C), e.g. one for 3-6-month-olds, one for 7-12-month-olds, and one for 12-18-month-olds.

45. D: In DRAs, students follow up reading with workbook and/or other practice activities that help them to review vocabulary and their comprehension. Some reading selections can include enrichment activities that relate the reading to art, music, or drama (A) as well as to writing. Students do read silently (B) and then read aloud. Teachers introduce them to new concepts and vocabulary words before they read text, not after (C).

46. C: Tier-two words. Tier-two words are words that are used with high frequency across a variety of disciplines or words with multiple meanings. They are characteristic of mature language users. Knowing these words is crucial to attaining an acceptable level of reading comprehension and communication skills.

47. C: Preschool IQ scales and similar standardized assessment instruments typically involve more complicated procedures, like weighting individual item values; converting raw scores to standard scores/percentages; reversing some items' point values; and comparing student scores to national norms in tables provided with tests. By contrast, paper-and-pencil self-reporting surveys/questionnaires often require only adding up item points for a total score (A); or adding up values within sections for a group of scores (B). Some screening tools require only noting whether the child's score passes the cut-off value indicating need for assessment (D).

48. D: Teachers will observe a variety of developmental arcs when teaching reading since all students learn differently. It is very important to understand which instances are normal in the course of learning and which signal a learning difficulty. Barrett is still exhibiting confusion over certain letter-sounds, typically when the letters look similar. At his age, this difficulty could suggest that Barrett has an issue with reading that could be addressed by a reading specialist. The other three choices describe normal behaviors that are commonly exhibited by children when they are learning to read. Choice C, Noelle, may describe an instance in which a student is having a learning problem. However, the teacher will need more information about Noelle's reading skills besides her reluctance to read before making a determination about how to proceed.

49. C: Are homophones. Homophones are words that are pronounced the same but differ in meaning. For example, a bride wears a 2 caret ring, but a horse eats a carrot. These words are not all nouns or monosyllabic, and none of them are dipthongs. Dipthongs (D) are a single-syllable sound made up by combining two vowels, such as in the words *weird*, *applause*, and *boy*.

50. C: Printed mathematical formulas are an example of abstract mathematical concepts presented abstractly. Young children cannot access such concepts in abstract presentations. However, they can learn to understand abstract concepts when they are presented using concrete manipulatives like tangrams for shape recognition (A), or for reproducing and designing patterns, solving spatial problems, etc.; large, magnetized numbers and number boards (B) for doing math computations concretely; play money and toy cash registers (D) for monetary numerical activities; linking cubes, color tiles; and many other math manipulatives, which are available for teachers/schools to purchase, and/or which teachers can create in homemade versions using common found objects.

51. B: The Bank Street Developmental Interaction approach to early childhood education believes that children develop self-discipline and self-control through growing up in the controlled environments it provides. These controlled environments require all teachers to create well-designed classrooms; hence (A) is incorrect. Bank Street emphasizes the importance of giving children transitions between activities; hence, (C) is incorrect. This approach also stresses changing learning subjects at regular time intervals to foster children's developing a sense of direction and taking responsibility for what they do; hence (D) is incorrect.

52. D: The MLA guidelines for citing multiple authors of the same work in in-text citations (for both print and online sources) dictate using the first author's name plus "et al" for the other authors when there are four or more authors. If there are two (options A and B) or three (options B and C) authors, the guidelines say to name each author, either in a signal phrase [for example, "Smith and Jones note that... (45)" or "Smith, Jones, and Gray have noted... (45)"] or in a parenthetical reference ["(Smith, Jones, and Gray 45)."].

53. A: The /p/ sound is among the earliest phonemes to develop, from ages 1.5 to 3 years old. The /ʒ/ phoneme (B) has the oldest age norm for normal development—5.5 years to 8.5 years old is a typical range for children to acquire correct production of this sound. The /v/ sound (C) typically develops in most children from the ages of 4 to 8 years. Most children develop correct articulation of the /s/ sound (D) by 2.5 to 4 years old. Hence, not all kindergarteners, who are typically around 5 years old, are expected to master phonemes with acquisition norm ranges older than 5-8 years. A 5-year-old is *most* likely to be referred for SLP evaluation if s/he does not correctly produce /p/, which children normally develop by around 3 years old.

54. C: Froebel believed teacher-student relationships should be equal rather than authoritarian; and parents, particularly mothers, should be engaged and collaborate in children's education; so (D) is incorrect. Froebel observed that drawing and other art activities developed higher-order cognitive skills, so (A) is incorrect. Froebel believed that children's games taught virtues, so (B) is incorrect.

55. A: In Montessori Method schools, Early Childhood-aged students learn subject matter in science, art, music, movement, time, history, geography, and zoology. They may be exposed to various cultures and languages; however, they do NOT all* learn to converse in several different languages as a group. (*Individual children's interests guide Montessori learning. As the Michael Olaf Montessori Company states, "....A child can work on any material he understands at any time.") The other answer choices all describe activities included in each of the corresponding areas.

56. D: Rate, accuracy, and prosody. Fluent readers are able to read smoothly and comfortably at a steady pace (rate). The more quickly a child reads, the greater the chance of leaving out a word or substituting one word for another (for example, *sink* instead of *shrink*). Fluent readers are able to maintain accuracy without sacrificing rate. Fluent readers also stress important words in a text, group words into rhythmic phrases, and read with intonation (prosody).

57. A: It is a standard of Information Literacy (IL) that students must use their own critical thinking skills to evaluate the quality of the information and its sources before they use it. Another standard is that the student should ascertain how much information s/he needs for his/her purposes first; deciding this after uncovering excessive information is inefficient (B). An additional IL standard is to access necessary information in an efficient and effective way. However, none of these standards include the idea that students will lose incidental learning or broadness of scope by doing so (C). IL standards include the principle that students *should* use the information they find in ways that are effective for attaining their specific purposes (D).

58. A: Mnemonic devices are a way to aid in memorization. The concept to be memorized is linked to a device: an easily remembered song, saying, or image. To remember the concept, one needs only to remember the device.

59. C: Scientific knowledge is not one of the domains included in the SECI as predictive of kindergarten readiness. The SECI assesses young children's progress in the domains of mathematics (A), alphabet knowledge (B), phonological awareness (D), and oral language development.

60. A: When choosing screening and assessment instruments, EC program administrators should look for tests that measure the same developmental areas/domains that their programs use. The tests they use should also support the goals established by their programs (B). The administration, scoring, and interpretation methods used by each test should be congruent with the skills of the program's staff (C). Administrators should also select instruments that are proven to be statistically valid and reliable (D).

61. C: Once the students' notecards have been checked and edited for accuracy, they can easily be used to demonstrate the process of organizing ideas in an essay or research paper. Students can use their notecards as aids for making their outlines. They simply have to arrange the notecards in an appropriate order and add pertinent information to bridge the ideas together in their writing.

62. B: Programs that promote general EC development, like Head Start, should select comprehensive assessment instruments to test overall child development. Outreach programs that seek to identify children with untreated/undetected mental health disorders (A) should choose instruments for assessing social-emotional development rather than temperament. Clinics that specialize in treating children with regulatory disorders (C) could benefit from choosing tests that measure temperament rather than social-emotional development. Prevention programs that help multi-need families access supports and services (D) would do better to use measures for risk and resiliency factors than combinations of several tests, which are better for use by multi-faceted ECE programs than risk and resiliency measures would be.

63. B: Researchers have found that the writing processes both form a hierarchy and are observably recursive in nature. Moreover, they find that when students continually revise their writing, they are able to consider new ideas and to incorporate these ideas into their work. Thus, they do not merely correct mechanical errors when revising (A), they also add to the content and quality of their writing. Furthermore, research shows that writers, including students, not only revise their actual writing; during rewrites, they also reconsider their original writing goals rather than always retaining them (C), and they revisit their prewriting plans rather than leaving these unaffected in rewriting (D).

64. B: The whole language approach to early childhood literacy instruction puts emphasis on helping children to create meaning from what they read, and also to express meaning in what they write (C). This approach additionally does emphasize cultural diversity (A). It places importance on reading children's literature of high quality (D).

65. B: Research finds positive reinforcement—presenting a reward immediately after a behavior to increase it—more powerful than all other techniques. People are highly motivated by rewards. Negative reinforcement (A)—removing something someone doesn't like to increase a behavior—is not as effective as positive reinforcement, because people prefer the pleasure of getting something they like over the relief of getting rid of something they don't. Positive punishment (C)—presenting something someone doesn't like to decrease a behavior—and negative punishment (D)—removing something someone likes to decrease a behavior—are less effective because behaviors meet needs: punishment may suppress one behavior, but other behaviors emerge to meet the need. For example, children misbehaving for attention regard even punishments like scolding as attention. Punishment is also limited: not applied consistently, it loses effect; children can react differently to punishments from different teachers; and punishment can cause children's fear/anger/defiance/resentment.

66. D: Emergent literacy theory incorporates influences from Piaget and Vygotsky, who both described reading and writing as developmental processes that go through successive, discrete stages. Emergent literacy theorists have done extensive research and found that when young children "reread" storybooks, this does not mean they have memorized them (A) but rather that they are reconstructing the books' meanings. Research also finds that young children's invented spellings do afford information about their familiarity with specific phonetic components of words (B). Emergent literacy theorists find it crucial for adults to read to young children regardless of how young they are (C).

67. C: Covalent. Covalent compounds are usually formed by the combination of two or more non-metallic elements with one another. In these compounds atoms share electrons. Ionic compounds are most often formed between a metal and a non-metal. Organic compounds are covalent compounds which contain carbon and hydrogen atoms. "Chemical compounds" is a general term that can mean any type of compound, either ionic or covalent.

68. D: Sound cannot travel through a vacuum, though it doesn't necessarily follow that it *can* travel through solids. Nor does the fact sound can travel through a solid follow from the fact that the atoms are packed tightly together. The fact that a sound is produced by knocking on a solid object also does not prove sound can pass through the object. However, if you hear a sound on the other side of a solid wall, the sound must have traveled through the wall. Choice D is the best answer.

69. B: Cool the liquid. If a gas and a liquid are placed in a sealed container, cooling the liquid will help dissolve the gas into the liquid. Gasses have higher solubility in liquids at lower temperatures. At higher temperatures, the gas molecules will have more kinetic energy and will have enough energy to overcome intermolecular interactions with the liquid solvent and leave the solution. This also explains why heating the liquid is incorrect. Shaking the container is also incorrect as this would give the gas energy to escape. Decreasing the pressure on the lid may or may not significantly affect the pressure inside the vessel depending on the nature of the vessel, but decreasing the pressure inside the vessel would decrease the solubility of the gas in the liquid.

70. C: Vinegar fizzing when poured on a rock is an example of chemical weathering. Mechanical and chemical weathering are processes that break down rocks. Mechanical weathering breaks down rocks physically but does not change their chemical composition. Frost and abrasion are examples. Water, oxygen, carbon dioxide and living organisms can lead to the chemical weathering of rock. Vinegar is a weak acid and will undergo a chemical reaction, evidenced by fizzing, with the rock. Rain freezing on the roadway is an example of the phase change of water from a liquid to a solid and may lead to physical weathering. Ivy growing on the side of a wooden house is incorrect since the house is not a rock. A river carrying sediment downstream is an example of erosion.

71. D: There may be a different number of atoms for the products and the reactants. This is not true of a chemical reaction. Chemical equations must be balanced on each side of the reaction. Balancing means the total number of atoms stays the same, but their arrangement within specific reactants and products can change. The law of conservation of matter states that matter can never be created or destroyed. Heat may be absorbed or released in a reaction; these are classified as endothermic and exothermic reactions, respectively. The rate of the reaction increases with temperature for most reactions.

72. A: The distance from the Earth to the Sun is equal to one astronomical unit. An astronomical unit (AU) is equal to 93 million miles and is far smaller than a light year or a parsec. A light year is defined as the distance light can travel in a vacuum in one year, and is equal to roughly 64,341 AU. A parsec is the parallax of one arcsecond and is equal to 206.26×10^3 astronomical units.

63

73. C: Igneous rock. Fossils are least likely to be found in igneous rock. Igneous rock is formed by extreme heat as magma escapes through the Earth's crust and cools. The remains of plants and animals in fossil form are not usually preserved under these conditions. Sedimentary rock is where the abundance of fossils are found. Sedimentary rock is formed more slowly and is very abundant. Since soft mud and silts compress into layers, organisms can also be deposited. Metamorphic rock is rock that has undergone change by heat and pressure. This usually destroys any fossils, but occasionally fossil remains are distorted and can be found in metamorphic rock.

74. D: Voltage is the same for each path and current is greatest in path C. In a parallel circuit, the voltage is the same for all three paths. Because the resistance is different on each path but the voltage is the same, Ohm's law dictates that the current will also be different for each path. Ohm's law says that current is inversely related to resistance. Therefore, the current will be greatest in path C as it has the least resistance, 2 ohms.

75. D: Its temperature remains the same due to the latent heat of fusion. The temperature of a substance during the time of any phase change remains the same. In this case, the phase change was from liquid to solid, or freezing. Latent heat of fusion, in this case, is energy that is released from the substance as it reforms its solid form. This energy will be released and the liquid will turn to solid before the temperature of the substance will decrease further. If the substance were changing from solid to liquid, the heat of fusion would be the amount of heat required to break apart the attractions between the molecules in the solid form to change to the liquid form. The latent heat of fusion is exactly the same quantity of energy for a substance for either melting or freezing. Depending on the process, this amount of heat would either be absorbed by the substance (melting) or released (freezing).

76. A: A correlational study of a population is an example of a descriptive study. Choices B and C are examples of the controlled experimentation type of scientific investigation. Choice D is an example of the comparative data analysis type of scientific investigation.

77. C: Tropical climate zones are characterized by frequent rainfall, especially during the monsoon season, and by moderate temperatures that vary little from season to season or between night and day. Tropical zones do experience frequent rainfall, which leads to abundant vegetation.

78. D: Theory. Once a hypothesis has been verified and accepted, it becomes a theory. A theory is a generally accepted explanation that has been highly developed and tested. A theory can explain data and be expected to predict outcomes of tests. A fact is considered to be an objective and verifiable observation; whereas, a scientific theory is a greater body of accepted knowledge, principles, or relationships that might explain a fact. A law is an explanation of events by which the outcome is always the same. A conclusion is more of an opinion and could be based on observation, evidence, fact, laws, or even beliefs.

79. B: It is true that rocks are classified by their formation and the minerals they contain, while minerals are classified by their chemical composition and physical properties. Choice A is incorrect because rocks may contain traces of organic compounds. Choices C and D are incorrect because only minerals can be polymorphs and only rocks contain mineraloids.

80. D: Decay. The process whereby a radioactive element releases energy slowly over a long period of time to lower its energy and become more stable is best described as decay. The nucleus undergoing decay, known as the parent nuclide, spontaneously releases energy most commonly through the emission of an alpha particle, a beta particle or a gamma ray. The changed nucleus, called the daughter nuclide, is now more stable than the parent nuclide, although the daughter nuclide may undergo another decay to an even more stable nucleus. A decay chain is a series of decays of a radioactive element into different more stable elements.

81. D: The asteroid belt in our solar system is located between Mars and Jupiter. The asteroid belt is populated by asteroids and dwarf planets that are distributed thinly enough that spacecraft can pass through the belt with relative ease.

82. A: Heat on Earth is generated by the Sun. The more direct sunlight an area on Earth receives from the Sun, the warmer it will be. The earth is most tilted towards or away from the sun at the solstices between spring and summer or between fall and winter. When the Northern hemisphere is tilted away from the Sun, all of the countries in the Northern hemisphere experience fall and winter. At that same time, the Southern hemisphere experiences spring and summer. The same is true when the Southern hemisphere experiences fall and winter; the Northern hemisphere experiences spring and summer.

83. C: The slope is very steep. On a topographic map, an area where the contour lines are very close together indicates that the slope is very steep. Lines very far apart would indicate a more gradual change in elevation. Contour lines help represent the actual shape of the Earth's surface features and geographic landmarks like rivers, lakes and vegetation. Topographic maps also show man-made features such as roads, dams, and major buildings. They are based on aerial photography and the quadrangle maps are produced in various scales. The 7.5-minute quadrangle is very common and provides a 1:24,000 scale, where 1 inch represents 2,000 feet.

84. C: Research has found significant variations among parental age expectations for various EC developmental milestones (e.g., weaning, eating, toilet-training, dressing, sleeping, etc.). Thus what is normal for one culture is abnormal for another. For example, Anglo parents usually introduce and encourage drinking from a cup to one-year-olds, so an eighteen-month-old not doing this could signal some developmental delay; but Filipino parents normally have not even introduced a cup to eighteen-month-olds, so their not using cups is developmentally normal. As in this example, some developmental milestones not reached by a certain age is *not* always a cause for concern (D). Assessment data *are* more likely to be misinterpreted when the educators' and parents' cultures differ (A) than when they share a common culture. Although age expectations for milestones vary across cultures, educators *cannot* automatically attribute everything to this variation when a child could also need a complete developmental assessment (B).

85. B: One factor educators must consider about immigrant parents is that they may not be aware of what special education and/or supplemental services are available to their children in American schools. Thus they are not negligent or refusing to request such services, but need to be informed about them, which educators must do. Culturally diverse parents and educators are likely to disagree about some educational goals for children, but educators should collaborate with parents to further those goals they both agree on rather than trying to convince parents to agree (A) on all goals. Educators should also remember that immigrant parents' not advocating for their children to receive needed services is not necessarily due to lack of interest (C) or resistance to confronting problems (D). In addition to lacking information, some parents from cultures with more paternalistic educational systems are trained *not* to speak up, but to wait for educators to raise concerns before expressing children's problems they have witnessed.

86. C: Lying at a little more than 23° south of the equator, the Tropic of Capricorn is the border between the Southern Temperate Zone to the south and the Tropical Zone to the north. The southern hemisphere is tilted toward the sun to its maximum extent each year at the winter solstice in December. The northernmost latitude at which the sun can appear directly overhead is at the

Tropic of Cancer during the summer solstice. The northern and southern hemispheres are separated by the equator at 0° degrees latitude. The eastern and western hemispheres are separated by the prime meridian at 0° longitude.

87. B: Paul Revere and William Dawes were both dispatch riders who set out on horseback from Massachusetts to spread news of British troop movements across the American countryside around the beginning of the War of Independence. John Parker was the captain of the Minutemen militia, who were waiting for the British at Lexington, Massachusetts.

88. D: Individualistic cultures, like that of the United States, value scientific thinking and object manipulation as skills to teach young children. Individualism favors the independence of each person, individuals realizing their full potential (self-actualization), and distinguishing themselves from the group. Collectivism favors the interdependence (C) of individuals and their social relationships, interactions, and connections. Collectivist cultures value cooperation to achieve group harmony (B), while individualist cultures value competition among group members to achieve individual excellence.

89. C: There are no formal qualifications for members of the judicial branch. However, having a background in law is an informal qualification that is considered when appointing Article III judges.

90. B: Researchers have found that Hispanic families in the U.S. are more likely to choose home- and family-based child care and preschool education than outside centers. This may reflect the collectivist nature of Latin culture, which values social interactions and relationships more than structure. Caucasian parents in the U.S. are found to prefer preschool centers. This reflects not only the North American culture's individualistic emphasis on structured early learning, and predominant North American custom, but also North American Caucasian parents' attention to scientific findings that center-based preschool education improves children's school readiness skills.

91. C: Physical geography focuses on processes and patterns in the natural environment. What people eat in any given geographic region is largely dependent on such environmental factors as climate and the availability of arable land. Religion, family, and language may all be affected by geographical factors, but they are not as immediately affected as dietary preferences.

92. B: The Seven Years War was a global military conflict. In the Americas, the conflict was largely between Western European countries, Great Britain and France, in particular.

93. A: The inaccurate statement is the Puritans unconditionally supported the English Reformation. While they agreed with the Reformation in principle, they felt that it had not pursued those principles far enough and should make greater reforms. Similarly, they felt that the Church of England (or Anglican Church), though it had separated from the Catholic Church in the Protestant Reformation, still allowed many practices they found too much like Catholicism (B). The Puritans did become a chief political power in England because of the first English Civil War (C) between Royalists and Parliamentarians. The Royalists had a profound suspicion of the radical Puritans. Among the Parliament's elements of resistance, the strongest was that of the Puritans. They joined in the battle initially for ostensibly political reasons as others had, but soon they brought more attention to religious issues. Following the Restoration in 1660 and the Uniformity Act of 1662, thereby restoring the Church of England to its pre-English Civil War status, the great majority of Puritan clergy defected from the Church of England (D). It is also accurate that the Puritans in England disagreed about separating from the Church of England. Some Puritans desired complete separation; they were known first as Separatists and after the Restoration as Dissenters. Others did not want complete separation but instead desired further reform in the Church of England. While they remained part of the Church of England, they were called Non-Separating Puritans, and after the Restoration, they were called Nonconformists.

94. A: The eye wall of a hurricane has the strongest winds and the greatest rainfall. The eye wall is the tower-like rim of the eye. It is from this wall that clouds extend out, which are seen from above as the classic outward spiral pattern. A hurricane front is the outermost edge of its influence; although there will be heavy winds and rain in this area, the intensity will be relatively small. The eye of a hurricane is actually a place of surprising peace. In this area, dry and cool air rushes down to the ground or sea. Once there, the air is caught up in the winds of the eye wall and is driven outward at a furious pace.

95. C: In family systems theory, the family climate refers to the family's physical and emotional environment and emotional quality. Climate affects a child's feelings of safety or fear, support or rejection, and feeling loved or unloved. Hierarchy (A) refers to the family's balance of power, decision making, and control, which can change with changes in family makeup and is affected by factors like socioeconomic status, age, gender, religion, and culture. Boundaries (B) refer to the family's limits and definitions of togetherness and separateness, and what the family excludes or includes. Equilibrium (D) refers to the family's consistency or balance, which is preserved through family customs, traditions, and rituals, and disrupted by changes and stressors.

96. D: Area differentiation in geography refers to regional variations in occupations. It also refers to regional variations in geographical characteristics; e.g., people grow different plants in highlands than in lowlands according to what grows best in their respective altitudes and climates. (A) is an example of the geographical concept of utility value, i.e., how much use natural resources are to different people—oceans have more utility value for fishermen than farmers, while forests have more utility value for naturalists than academics. (B) is an example of the geographical concept of spatial interrelatedness, i.e., the relationship of geographic phenomena and non-physical characteristics like rural or urban regions. (C) is an example of the geographical concept of agglomeration, i.e., the tendency of people and their settlements and activities to concentrate in the most profitable areas.

97. D: In the Dred Scott decision of 1857, the Court ruled that no slave or descendant of slaves could ever be a United States citizen. It also declared the Missouri Compromise of 1820 to be unconstitutional, clearing the way for the expansion of slavery in new American territories. This ruling pleased Southerners and outraged the North further dividing the nation and setting the stage for war.

98. C: The Mason-Dixon Line was the manifestation of a border dispute between Great Britain and the colonists. It effectively separated, or illustrated, a cultural divide between North and South before the Civil War.

99. A: The Age of Enlightenment was a time of scientific and philosophical achievement. Also called the Age of Reason, it was a time when human thought and reason were prized.

100. A: Rivers promoted the development of the ancient river valley civilizations of the world, including in the Middle East, India, and China. Rivers not only supply water for drinking and crop irrigation; they also provide fertile soil, vegetation for shade cover, food, building materials, and animal life. They additionally allow water travel to other locations. Although some peoples have settled and lived in deserts, they are among the most inhospitable climates. Forests also provide plenty of flora and fauna and exist in areas receiving enough rainfall, but rivers have been

historically superior in attracting human societies. Mountains near living areas provide protective barriers; however, though some peoples live there, as in deserts, living in the mountains is difficult due to high altitudes, harsh climates, poor soil for planting, and rough terrain.

Thank You

We at Mometrix would like to extend our heartfelt thanks to you, our friend and patron, for allowing us to play a part in your journey. It is a privilege to serve people from all walks of life who are unified in their commitment to building the best future they can for themselves.

The preparation you devote to these important testing milestones may be the most valuable educational opportunity you have for making a real difference in your life. We encourage you to put your heart into it—that feeling of succeeding, overcoming, and yes, conquering will be well worth the hours you've invested.

We want to hear your story, your struggles and your successes, and if you see any opportunities for us to improve our materials so we can help others even more effectively in the future, please share that with us as well. **The team at Mometrix would be absolutely thrilled to hear from you!** So please, send us an email (support@mometrix.com) and let's stay in touch.

If you feel as though you need additional help, please check out the other resources we offer:

Study Guide: http://MometrixStudyGuides.com/MTEL

Flashcards: http://MometrixFlashcards.com/MTEL